CREATIVE
HOMEOWNER®

The Best of
Signature Kitchens

CREATIVE HOMEOWNER®, Upper Saddle River, New Jersey

First published in book form in 2005 by

CRE▲TIVE
HOMEOWNER®

A Division of Federal Marketing Corp.
Upper Saddle River, NJ

Text and photos © 2004 Magnolia Media Group

Signature Kitchens & Baths Magazine is published by Magnolia Media Group

VP/Editorial Director: Timothy O. Bakke
Production Manager: Kimberly H. Vivas

Art Director: David Geer
Book Layout: Kamal Mahtani
Cover Design: David Geer

Printed in China

Current Printing (last digit)
10 9 8 7 6 5 4 3 2 1

The Best of Signature Kitchens
Library of Congress
Catalog Card Number: 2004099813
ISBN: 1-58011-251-X

CREATIVE HOMEOWNER®
A Division of Federal Marketing Corp.
24 Park Way
Upper Saddle River, NJ 07458
www.creativehomeowner.com

Contents

Some Basics

The Kitchens

Appendix

This paint and hand-glazed kitchen was custom manufactured by Royal Cabinet Company. The top-to-bottom use of carved ornamentation embellishes the kitchen with classical detailing. To add color, a Jerusalem Gold marble was selected for the island as an offset to the Uba Tuba granite tops of the periphery. The homeowner's large collection of china is beautifully displayed in two glass front armoires.

These custom cabinets were created by Atwood Fine Architectural Cabinetry of Birmingham, Mich.

CABINETRY:
Adding a Touch of Sophistication to Any Room

WHETHER YOU ARE DESIGNING A NEW KITCHEN OR REMODELING, CHOICES OF CABINETS CAN BE OVERWHELMING. DECIDE ON WHAT FEATURES YOU TRULY NEED AND WILL USE ON A DAILY BASIS. TEXTURE, COLOR AND DURABILITY SHOULD BE NOTED WHEN SHOPPING FOR NEW CABINETS. WHEN IT DOES

comes to durability keep your family in mind too. Is your lifestyle full of children running from activity to activity, splashing food all over? Or do you only entertain when you must, like when family comes over? Lifestyle can be a big factor when choosing cabinets for any room of the house, even the outdoors.

Function, a stylish look, safety, warm cozy colors and outdoor options are just a few new categories cabinetmakers are considering for you when designing a new series.

Storing Function
Being able to put things into other things is so much fun, especially when the storage itself is beautiful, durable and long-lasting.

Canyon Creek Cabinet Company has announced the addition of a new drawer box system. The new system replaces their particleboard construction drawer box with a wood veneer plywood and features concealed, epoxy-coated under-mount guides. The new self-closing drawer system provides wider drawers with added strength

and durability and is made available to customers at no extra charge.

The vast combination of unique storage and design options from Quality Custom Cabinetry provide unending possibilities for kitchen, bath and custom home environments. Corner alcoves, cooking center mantels and armoire cabinets that conceal microwaves, TVs and small appliances create kitchen designs that are as efficient as they are beautiful. Decorative options include custom islands, unique wall cabinetry and cabinetry with the look of freestanding furniture.

Wellborn Cabinet, Inc., has added more than 125 new sizes and accessories to an already spectacular product line. New options in the Premier and WoodCraft Series to help you get organized include the Blind Corner Base with Pull-out Tray, which is ideal for organizing canned goods and non-perishables in the most convenient locations.

The calm, simple, streamlined interior spaces of Plain & Fancy's Softer Spartan line will help you organize your fast and furious lifestyle. Though sophisticated and modern, at its core, Softer Spartan demonstrates the movement towards living tastefully while maintaining warmth and balance.

Yorktowne Cabinets continues to enhance its new products programs with new sizes that are designed to give consumers what they want in both form and function. Some of the company's new introductions include a mini-pantry storage unit that takes only 9 or 12 inches of wall space; a 6-inch wide apothecary spice drawer; and pullouts that turn filler into functional storage space.

Style

In recent years, home remodeling, renovation and decoration have experienced a significant upswing, as consumers spend more time in their homes and with their families. Consumers are finding that Diamond Cabinetry provides the perfect combination of attractive cabinetry styles with unique storage options.

Diamond Logix, an array of innovative storage options, provides solutions for a wide range of lifestyles. In developing the Logix line, according to brand manager Tara Eckman, Diamond researched trends and talked with consumers, including gourmet cooks, avid entertainers and families with young children. The company asked about the storage needs of people who entertain regularly, and created options to accommodate serving trays, table linens and wine glasses. After interviews with cooking enthusiasts, Diamond developed storage to organize utensils and cabinets with rollout shelves to keep pots and pans within easy reach.

In addition to the vast array of Logix storage innovations, Diamond Cabinetry currently offers more than 200 door style and finish combinations, making it easy for designers and homeowners to create exactly the cabinetry they envisioned.

The latest introductions to Habersham Furniture Company's growing line of upscale designs for the kitchen and bath have received an enthusiastic response from retailers, certified kitchen and bath designers, and builders. Among the introductions were new islands, commodes, vanities, as well as other designs reflecting Habersham's signature Old World European style in practical designs.

Before developing its new line Logix line, Diamond Cabinetry researched trends and talked to countless consumers about their storage needs. The results are pots and pans within easy reach.

"Kitchen and bath décor is becoming increasingly important in the minds of today's homeowner," said Joyce Eddy, chairman/founder of Habersham. "Consumers are looking for original pieces that reflect the look of the whole house, yet are practical for their lifestyle."

With its contrasting dark wood top and distressed, cream-colored base, the Breakfast Bar is a beautiful yet functional piece for the kitchen. Adding a raised bar area to a traditional kitchen island, Habersham has created a casual dining area paired with additional work space, perfect for the larger kitchens of today's expansive homes. This grand scale piece features three drawers, two storage compartments underneath and two shelves at each end of the piece.

Shenandoah Cabinetry has introduced the Breckenridge Collection, which includes glazed doors, custom finishes and the sophistication of hardwoods. The glazed finishes are created with a final tint using a contrasting semi-transparent stain. The additional color highlights the recessed areas while the flat areas take on a richer look. The overall effect is the mark of custom craftsmanship and highlights the nuances and beauty of the elegant and classic cabinet.

No More Ouchies!

We have all had our fingers and hands smashed in the cabinet door as they are closing. Now this little problem has been solved with a new line from Quality Custom Cabinetry. Quality Custom Cabinetry's Safety Susan base corner revolving storage prevents pinched fingers. As the door opens, the revolving unit recesses approximately one inch from the doorframe into the cabinet interior. This extra clearance space assures greater safety than standard lazy Susan designs. It is especially desirable in avoiding finger "ouchies" for small children.

Quality Custom Cabinetry offers the Safety Susan for its exclusive line of custom cabinetry styles and finishes. The consistently precise fit is in keeping with the old world workmanship of Quality Custom Cabinetry. Durable Safety Susan construction provides sturdy storage with smooth, quiet operation.

A Forest of Choices

With so many homes being custom built today, why not have your cabinets custom built as well? With more than 50 years of successfully working with homeowners, Holiday Kitchens helps determine not only a family's needs by understanding its lifestyle. No two families are alike, so no two kitchens can be built the same way. The company's solutions are as numerous as their cabinets, and each hardwood has its own unique personality. There area enough differences in color, grain, and texture that you're sure to find one wood, or several, to match you personal taste and decorating preferences for your cabinetry. From the coarse texture of red oak to the straight-grained texture of maple, Holiday offers a variety of customizable options for every homeowner.

One company is offering hundreds of style combinations by merging with another. Omega Cabinetry is turning the cost/quality equation on its head by coordinating two lines, Dynasty and Omega Custom. The interchangeability of these two lines gives homeowners complete semi-custom cabinetry options and the ability to upgrade to coordinated, fully custom cabinetry as they wish. Through Dynasty, the company offers 40 door styles in five wood species, including maple, oak, cherry, red birch and pecan. To these, the Omega Custom line adds walnut, rustic oak and rustic pecan. Each style has recommended overlay and drawer style, and these most popular choices are built into the affordable Dynasty line. At the same time, Omega Custom's additional options of four overlay styles, two inset styles and seven drawer fronts make it easy to design a truly unique

The Breakfast Bar from Habersham adds a casual dining area paired with additional workspace. The grand piece includes three drawers, two storage compartments and two shelves on either end.

Atwood Fine Architectural Cabinetry of Birmingham, Mich., created cabinets that not only complemented the kitchen décor, but also let the outdoors in.

kitchen or to give a special treatment to an island or focus-point cabinet.

Old World Charm Warms Up

Recent trends in home design are moving away from stark colors and toward warmer, lighter, more calming tones. In response to this trend, Diamond Cabinetry has developed two dazzling new maple finishes: toasted almond (a creamy, warm glaze) and harvest (a tawny, golden brown finish).

"We are seeing warmer colors throughout the house, especially in the kitchen," said Andy Well, director of product design for Diamond Cabinetry. The trend gives consumers a new palette of choices to help them create a timeless design.

Variety

When you begin exploring the possibilities for your kitchen, the options will begin to multiply exponentially. Medallion Cabinetry has 11 enticing door styles available in each of five different wood species, providing more than 800 wood door style and finish combinations from which to choose. The natural finish highlights the character of alder, cherry, hickory, maple and oak, and many decorative options are available, including specialty glass doors, appliqués, fluted pilasters and crown molding.

Outdoor World

Danver, the manufacturer of the Commercial Home Products line of stainless steel for the home, is expanding its stainless steel-clad five-ply wood kitchen cabinets to include outdoor use. In order to address the needs of designers for more flexibility when planning outdoor kitchens, as well as the demand for the stainless look outdoors, Danver has incorporated a new cabinet material that is impervious to the weather and insects.

Danver has worked cooperatively with nationally known executive chef, media personality and recognized kitchen design expert Chef J. Warren to develop a unique high-end look and style for an outdoor kitchen. The result is a "chef-inspired" line of outdoor cabinets and modules with the beauty of high-quality indoor cabinets in form and function, but can withstand the effects of the weather. The indoor style and theme are carried outside for a fluid and contiguous look and feel. "Outdoor living and entertaining have taken on a larger focus for the affluent household," said Warren. "Complete outdoor kitchen and entertainment modules are in demand by builders and kitchen designers as a result of lifestyle demands from their customers and clients. This is a national phenomenon, especially in year-round good weather locales. Stainless just makes sense outdoors."

After years of looking, the cabinetry industry now has In & Out Cabinetry to thank for their new line of outdoor designed cabinets. In & Out Cabinetry has two lines of outdoor cabinetry-the Signature series, which will last a lifetime and comes in many colors, and the Islander Series, which can be painted to match your décor. This cabinetry will not absorb water, rot, split, fade or swell out of shape. In & Out Cabinetry

has five door styles to choose from and the cabinetry comes in most standard sizes with stainless steel hinges, adjustable legs for easy installation on uneven surfaces and will withstand the elements. The fine cabinetry can be found in outdoor kitchens, pool areas, outdoor grill islands, yachts, hotels, medical offices, bars and industrial work areas.

South American Flavor

Guignard Mechanical Systems has announced the launch of a major new product line for the emerging outdoor market. The product line, Café Cabinets, features an innovative stainless steel platform that can ship flat and be assembled in minutes with a few common shop tools or be delivered assembled.

"Developing Café Cabinets was a natural extension of our custom stainless steel business unit. We have been building interior and exterior cabinets for residential and commercial installations for years. We wanted to develop a cabinet system that could incorporate beautiful materials and have a timeless look," said Randy Guignard, owner of GMS.

Architects, designers and customers will love the beautiful finishing options available for Café Cabinets. Teak tops, doors and end panels; Jatoba, an exclusive South American hardwood; and other weather resistant hardwoods are available. A solid marine-grade composite proven in the yachting industry is available in several UV-stable colors. Of course, many will prefer the clean lines of an all-stainless system. ◆

Walker Zanger includes classical designs to inspire Via Forte, a sublime collection of handcrafted, natural travertine.

MAKING A STATEMENT
ONE SURFACE AT A TIME:

COUNTERTOPS
&BACKSPLASHES

SO YOU'VE CHOSEN THE FLOORING AND THE CABINETS, AND YOU'VE EVEN SELECTED THE APPLIANCES. BUT WHAT WILL YOU PUT THEM ON TOP OF? THAT DEPENDS ON THE DESIGN OF THE KITCHEN AND ITS MAJOR USES IT WILL PROVIDE. STAINLESS STEEL IS ALWAYS A GOOD OPTION FOR A CLEAN AND

simple line. A wood butcher block makes the statement that plain marble or granite just can't achieve. Countertops, along with their counterpart backsplashes, are one of the final pieces of the kitchen puzzle that can put the exclamation point to your design.

Strong Surfaces

The new Swanstone Chesapeake vanity top is the latest addition to the growing line of vanity tops from Swanstone solid surfacing. Part of the company's American Classic Collection, this center bowl vanity

top offers consumers strength, balance and beauty with a functional design. The Chesapeake design offers a larger bowl, thicker edge and taller backsplash that will complement the look of any home or business. Molded into a single unit, the Chesapeake is ideal for either new construction or a remodeling project.

The American Classics Chesapeake center bowl vanity top is available in seven standard sizes that range from 25 inches up to 61 inches. All of these sizes are available in the full allowance of Swanstone colors. Swanstone is an authentic solid surface.

Color and texture run all the way through and cannot wear away. Being a solid surface material, Swanstone is resistant to cracking and crazing, a common problem with glazed products. Unlike most materials, such as natural granite, marble, laminates and cultured marble, minor scratches can be removed by using abrasive pads and cleaners or fine grit sandpaper, which returns Swanstone to its original luster. Swanstone also offers a limited lifetime warranty.

Workable Wood

At Michigan Maple Block, great care has gone into the selection of materials, craftsmanship and manufacturing of these tops. The countertops' rich appearance, distinctive grains, character marks and color variations are the purest expressions in nature. Just as no two trees are alike, no piece of wood in the fabrication of these quality tops looks exactly like another. No man-made material can duplicate hardwood's variety, natural integrity and authenticity. As with any natural wood product, it is not unusual for some areas to appear darker in color than others. These are naturally occurring characteristics.

These Butcher Block tops are intended to be used as true cutting surfaces. They are coated with an acrylic finish, Durakryl 102, which does not require any maintenance. It is not necessary to sand off this finish prior to using the top, as it is approved for food service use. The finish is formulated to repel most household solvents. Stains can be cleaned off with fingernail polish remover or bleach, neither of which can hurt the finish. Although the finish is durable, it will scratch.

Clean the top like you would any counter surface, not allowing water to remain on the block for any length of time. To help preserve your block if used as a cutting surface it would be advisable to periodically reseal only the area on which you cut. Mineral oil can be used. If it becomes necessary to refinish your block due to usage, sand off the finish and apply either an oil finish or reseal with "Good Stuff" Urethane Gel clear protective finish.

Versatile Quartz

Designing your dream home starts with the selection of the right materials, and that's where Silestone comes in. Silestone is the world's leading quartz surface, combining strength and beauty to create the ultimate surfacing material.

Ideal for kitchen countertops, bathroom vanity tops, shower wall cladding, flooring, tabletops and so much more, Silestone is a premium surfacing material that offers a unique mix of strength and elegance with no maintenance required.

Silestone is composed of 93 percent natural quartz, offering a sophisticated look and the cool feel of natural stone. And with more than 35 colors available, and virtually unlimited edge designs to choose from, Silestone offers something for everybody to love. Plus Silestone has the widest availability of any quartz surface in the world, with more than 2,000 retailers offering Silestone in the United States alone. And to top it all off, Silestone is priced competitive with other natural stones and even plastic surfaces that lack its durability and allure.

Continuing to offer industry firsts, Silestone by Cosentino recently unveiled the Catalonia Series of contemporary bathroom designs that provides the architectural and design market with "all-in-one" combinations of supports, countertops, mirrors, washbasins and fixtures for ease of selection and installation.

"Catalonia combines beautiful metal, ceramic and glass with the timeless elegance of Silestone quartz surfaces, resulting in a single bathroom element that can easily be included in any new home or remodeling project," said Isabel Martinez, product development manager for Cosentino USA. "Whether you want to streamline a small half-bath or give a sleek, modern appearance to an older bathroom, Catalonia is an elegant choice."

The Catalonia Series consists of three countertop/mirror/washbasin styles - called Tarraco, Barcino and Girona - featuring interchangeable fixtures. Vanity tops are available in more than 40 Silestone colors, including the six fresh pastel colors from the new Cielo Series: orange fuego, silver nube, blue cielo, amarillo sand, verde agua and white dune. Silestone's natural quartz surfaces are highly durable, scratch- and stain-resistant.

Customized Marble

Marble Builders, Inc. is an importer and manufacturer of quality prefabricated marble products from China. The company mainly fabricates fireplaces, vanity tops, consoles and columns. The craftsmanship of the products reaches the state-of-the-art standard, as do the selection of marbles sources from China, Italy, Turkey, India and Brazil.

Marble Builders' products are handmade to create a unique curve line or edge finishes that machine cannot complete. The vanity top is hand-carved from a piece of marble block to shape into a top and sink together; accompany with a multi-curve edge and an antique look floral wrought iron stand. All together it expresses an elegant, classic feeling that is much more than its worth.

From stylish fireplaces to elegant vanity tops, from classic columns to various consoles, the company's marble products are suitable for mid-level track homes up to upscale customhouses. They will even custom make the stone creations from your design.

Mainly Metal

Since 1944, Eskay Metal Fabricating has carried on the tradition of manufacturing quality custom metal products in stainless steel, brass, copper, aluminum and embossed metals. SpecialtyStainless.com was created to focus on providing the finest custom metal countertops, integral sinks and specialty cabinetry to the residential and commercial markets. For today's contemporary lifestyle the company offers many options to enhance your kitchen workspace, including custom stainless steel countertops with integral sinks and backsplashes; brass, copper and embossed countertops; custom cabinetry, wall shelves, wall panels and specialty items.

The Metropolitan Collection from dc designs includes solid aluminum, crisp machine-cut designs, these finishes make great complements to the stainless steel appliances popular in today's kitchen. From the neo-classical twist with natural materials like terra cotta and tumbled stone to urban-industrial textures of stained concrete as well as contemporary minimalism, you will be impressed with how well these tiles complement different aesthetics. The aluminum is anodized for corrosion resistance and fingerprint protection, and it comes in two different finishes - brushed or distressed. ◆

Sub-Zero's glass-front refrigerator proves a lovely aesthetic addition to the kitchen while also serving as the ultimate in food storage.

Put your
KITCHEN APPLIANCES
TO WORK

EVEN THE MOST ACCOMPLISHED CHEF CAN USE A LITTLE ASSISTANCE WHEN PREPARING A MEAL OR GETTING READY FOR A PARTY. ALTHOUGH WE CAN'T GIVE YOU AN EXTRA HAND, WE HAVE FOUND SOME GREAT APPLIANCES THAT WILL MAKE YOUR TIME IN THE KITCHEN MUCH EASIER AND MORE ENJOYABLE.

Keeping It Cold

Never again will you have to settle for function over form. Some of the newer refrigeration models are proving that smarts and good looks can come in one package.

The new 650G refrigerator from Sub-Zero includes a large-capacity refrigeration space plus a generous-size freezer space and ice maker in the two-tier pullout drawer below. Electronic controls offer more accurate temperature adjustment, maintaining the temperature to plus or minus one degree of the owner's choice. Glass doors

allow a subdued interior light to glow softly with the door shut, adding a warm effect to the kitchen. When the door is opened, the light switches to full illumination.

Northland's ProChef models have some of the larger true storage capacities of any product available. The sleek outer look—complete with brushed stainless steel finish—is enhanced by all-metal interior walls and inner door panels as well as solid powder coated steel shelves. And three separately controlled compartments (for refrigeration, freezing and icemaker) allow the

only precisely accurate to within 1 degree, it is also amazingly easy to use. The user can choose the food type to be cooked, and the oven selects the perfect time and temperature. The world's first programmable digital oven, the MasterChef stores more than 30 recipes so anyone in the family can duplicate them at a later date.

Precision in cooking makes every meal more delightful, and the new Gaggenau combination steam and convection oven provides a high level of precision. The oven uses steam to protect the natural freshness, texture and color of food, then utilizes convection to precisely control temperature and air-flow. The cook is allowed 10 professional options for cooking with steam, including roasting and baking, steaming, low-temperature steam cooking, and misting.

Above: Marvel's Luxury Series includes amenities like quick-chill sections and proper rack-canting and humidity control.
Below: Elegant French design and construction combine with the finest cooking appointments in Morice's Marengo gas range.

Above: The grace and style of Price Pfister's Parisa faucet shroud its capability as a true kitchen workhorse.
Below: Gaggenau's built-in steamer allows cooks to steam food or boil in water, wine or stock.

owner maximum management.

A basement level wine cellar may be the most desirable way to store vino, but in most homes it is an unfeasible feature. So many homeowners are turning to a more recent vintage of appliance—the wine refrigerator. KitchenAid's newest contribution to the category is the Architect Series Wine Cellar, which has a sleek, wraparound stainless steel finish and room for up to 60 bottles of wine. And the Tri-Zone Cooling System assures that every bottle is kept at the proper temperature, from the top rack where red wines stay at 60 degrees to the bottom where sparkling wines are 45 degrees.

When it comes to style, no one ever talks about the "little white dress." Black is the universal color of taste and sophistication, and now the Marvel Luxury Series of under-counter beverage refrigeration is available in seductive black glossy interiors. The new units transform the staid into the stylish and make the competition literally pale in comparison.

Having long ago set the standard for luxury cooking in France, Morice has introduced in the United States the hand-crafted Supreme French cooker. The new line includes the same cooking power as its top-of-the-line Grand Veneur cookers but in a size suited for almost any sophisticated kitchen and offers five burner configurations, two ovens and a 4.75-gallon steamer option.

Batting Cleanup
While food preparation may be a dream, the end result of a great meal can be a nightmare. Home chefs no longer dread the scouring of pans or the scrubbing of dishes because of fabulous new technology in sinks and dishwashers.

Homeowners have the best of both fashion and performance

A Cooking Assistant
Miele's new MasterChef oven series is not

with the Price Pfister Marielle and Parisa kitchen pullout faucets. The new innovative design marries style with a three-function ergonomic spray head that doesn't sacrifice fashion or function. Artfully concealed in the spray head are push-button controls that activate a choice of three spray selections, making it a breeze to toggle between spray and stream modes with the flip of a finger.

Known as one of the quieter dishwashers on the market, Bosch has raised the bar yet again with the launch of its new product lineup featuring Apexx wash technology. The new line uses soil sensors to adjust wash cycle time and an exclusive flow-control technology to adjust water temperature and consumption.

Above: Owners of Bosch models say the dishwashers are so quiet, they have to touch the machine to know it is running.

Getting the Heat Out of the Kitchen

Some days are just too warm for heating up the inside of the house, and others are just too beautiful to stay inside. For those days there are a variety of options for outdoor cooking.

The Vintage outdoor kitchen line gathers the best of elegance, firepower and amenities into one complete built-in collection, the heart and soul of which is a 56-inch gas grill. With special touches like a state-of-the-art ceramic under-fired infrared burner, professional smoke enhancer and an optional commercial griddle, this series is causing grill envy in even the most upscale neighborhoods.

Also in the Vintage line is the new Bartending Center, which features a number of host-friendly features, including a built-in sink and removable cutting board, a door section for tall bottles, and two drawers that can hold anything from beverages to fresh fruit.

And why cook outside if you have to keep running back inside the house to the refrigerator? The Marvel Outdoor Series models are built to weather the elements but also make a statement with stunning cabinets of rugged stainless steel. From built-in models to those on casters for free wheeling, there's a perfect unit for every outdoor entertainer.

So no matter what the meal or where the preparation begins (and ends), you can count on many exciting new gadgets, tools and appliances to make your job more pleasant, therefore your dining and entertaining more satisfying. ◆

The Vintage outdoor kitchen line gathers the best of the best in one complete, built-in collection. The outdoor grill (above) includes side burners and an optional commercial grill, while the bartending center (below) has an insulated ice center, sorted tray to keep condiments cool, and a raised shelf for beautiful presentation of glassware.

Photographer: Peter Ledwith

Space is a premium in a New York City kitchen.

park avenue
giants

The clients on this remodeling project were a husband and wife whose grown sons had left home, prompting the couple to move back to New York City from the spacious suburbs where they raised their family. They got lucky when they found this bright, sunny kitchen, which is very large by the city's standards, but it needed a makeover. The lady of the house loves to cook and entertain, so this room sees lots of action and has to be functional. She also is an interior decorator, so it has to be beautiful as well.

Designer Guita Behbin of Dura Maid Industries knew it was important that the centerpiece island be proportional to the room but still allow ample aisle space. Therefore, Behbin created a multi-level island that facilitates traffic. The cabinet style is formal and is further dressed up with raised panels on the ends and columns on either side of the sink cabinet, range and holding up the eating counter. A double layer of crown molding above the

cabinets and at the ceiling carries the same cream color and black glaze as is on the cabinetry. Cabinets are of varied height for visual interest.

Additional interest comes from a graceful wood hood above the large, industrial-style range, as well as the backsplash tile, which carries a flower arrangement motif above the range.

What you don't see in this kitchen: the dishwasher, as a cabinet panel covers the appliance. What you do see: form and function extraordinaire.◆

Special Features:
Multi-level island; decorative wood hood with matching cabinets; column accents; oak flooring; Vermont Verde marble countertops

Dimensions:
15'6" x 16'

Products Used:
Cabinetry: Craft-Maid
Sink(s): Whitehaus
Faucets: Whitehaus
Dishwasher: Miele
Incognito
Refrigerator: Sub-Zero
Range: Viking

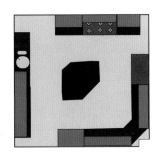

DESIGNER

Guita Behbin
Dura Maid Industries Inc.
130 Madison Ave.
New York, NY 10016
212.686.0246

Photographer: Oleg Marsh

All the amenities are squeezed into this small space.

cheery
co-op

This kitchen was part of a typical Manhattan postwar co-op apartment. The elderly couple lived there for years before deciding to renovate it to meet their needs and personal tastes. The room was quite small, with limited counter space and minimal storage. The clients, who cook a lot, needed a professional kitchen with full-size appliances and more storage and work space.

Incorporated into the original 9-by-7-foot galley were the cabinet and appliance portion of the kitchen. To create more storage space, designers installed an angled pantry next to the refrigerator, facing the adjoining dinette. In an unused corner of the room, occupied by steam pipes, designers created a broom closet. On the opposite wall, in the dinette, they placed a narrow countertop with shallow cabinets underneath and wall cabinets above.

In order to create additional architectural detail and to provide light for the kitchen, designers dropped the ceiling around the perimeter of the kitchen and installed recessed downlights. In the central part of the kitchen area, which was left at full height, Plexiglas supported by decorative crown molding covers a fluorescent fixture.

Cabinets are maple with a honey stain, which gives a warm and inviting feel. Three upper cabinets and the angled pantry have glass doors. Countertops and backsplashes are multicolored granite. A bright yellow checkerboard paper covers the walls. This combination of materials create a look that is both professional and cozy.◆

Special Features:
Dropped ceiling with raised part in center covered with Plexiglas imitating skylight; angled display cabinet with glass doors

Dimensions:
15' x 8'

Products Used:
Cabinetry: Regency Kitchens
Flooring: Vinyl tile
Countertops: International Stone and Accessories, multicolored granite
Sink(s): Franke PPX-110-21
Faucets: Franke FF300
Dishwasher: Miele 6870SC
Range: Dacor RSG30
Oven: MW JVM1190BY
Refrigerator: Sub-Zero 561

DESIGNER

Rochelle Kalisch, CKD
Regency Kitchens
204 E. 77th St.
New York, NY 10021
212.517.8707

4204 14th Ave.
Brooklyn, NY 11219
718.435.4266

An angled island offers easy access to every modern kitchen convenience.

old world
flair

Warm and inviting, with a pinch of old world flair, were just the right ingredients to create a successful kitchen remodel for this homeowner who loved to cook.

Don Boico, CKD, CR, of Classic Kitchen & Bath Center, accommodated the homeowner's love for cooking by including double ovens, a large Sub-Zero refrigerator, a double-bowl sink, and a five-burner gas cooktop in this classic kitchen remodel. Ample counter space,

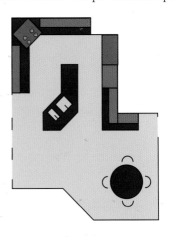

adjacent to the appliances and on the island, accommodates food preparation and clean-up tasks as well.

The angled island also serves to keep traffic out of the cook's work area. Family members can easily access the refrigerator for drinks and snacks, or carry a conversation with the cook, without interrupting meal preparation activities at the stove or sink.

There is no shortage of storage space in this dream kitchen. Roll-out shelves, dividers, and interior accessories combine to make cabinet contents easy to access, offering a place for everything from the tallest stock pot to the tiniest utensil.

Careful selection of materials results in a flawless combination of wood and natural stone. A well-designed lighting plan, including cove lighting above the cabinets and task lighting below them, complements the warm color palette, transforming this kitchen into a warm and inviting space where conversation is always welcome. ●

Special Features:
Angled island, fluted columns and a full-height granite backsplash create a hearth to house the cooktop, korbels and crown molding add design flair.

Dimensions:
15 feet by 18 feet

Products Used:
Cabinetry: Custom; Flooring: Pre-finished Limestone; Countertops: Granite; Sink(s): Franke; Faucets: Franke; Dishwasher: Bosch; Cooktop: Thermador; Refrigerator: Sub-Zero; Oven: Thermador; Microwave: General Electric.

DESIGNER

Don Boico, CKD, CR.
Contact Classic
Kitchen & Bath Center
Ltd., 1062 Northern
Blvd., Roslyn, NY
11576; 516/621-7700
or 60 B. Jobs Ln.,
Southampton, NY
11968; 631/204-9500

DESIGNER

Nick G. Virgilio.
Contact Janco Design
Group, Inc., 236 Crest
Ct., Bloomingdale, IL
60108; 630/529-2487

Photographer: Bill Richert

The kitchen, dining room and living room were combined to create a complete dining and social center all in one.

growing needs

Special Features:
Large multi-level island for seating, two ovens, "great room" design for entertaining.

Dimensions:
24 feet by 25 feet

Products Used:
Cabinetry: Merit; Flooring: Pergo; Countertops: Granite — yellow veniziano; Sink(s): Kindred; Dishwasher: Kitchen Aid; Cooktop: Kitchen Aid; Lighting: Task; Refrigerator: Kitchen Aid; Oven: Kitchen Aid; Microwave: Kitchen Aid; Compactor: Kitchen Aid.

The challenge presented to these long time homeowners and soon-to-be empty-nesters was how to accommodate their growing family get-togethers. With five grown children and an increasing number of grandchildren, seating for only seven was no longer enough. As a result, holidays and family functions were forced to spill over into the adjacent and separate dining room and living room.

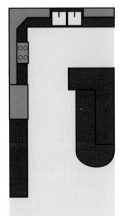

The solution was to carefully combine these three rooms, and Nick Virgilio, of Janco Design Group, Inc., rose to the challenge. A large structural beam concealed above the ceiling in the attic allowed Virgilio to remove the walls and create a completely open 25' x 24' great room on the main level of this split level home. This became a social center where meal preparation, dining and visiting can now occur simultaneously.

The old living room window now floods natural light onto a table suitable enough to seat ten. The large two level granite topped island offers seating for five more along with a large expanse for serving guests. A 42" refrigerator, two ovens and an abundance of cabinet storage meet the requirements for entertaining a large number of an ever-increasing list of family and friends. ●

DESIGNER

Michael Stockin, CKD.
Contact Kuntriset
Kitchens & Baths
Design Center, 5127
State Hwy. 12,
Norwich, NY 13815;
607/336-4197.

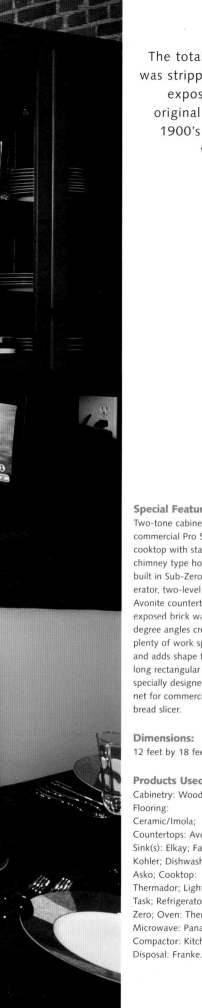

The total area was stripped to expose the original early 1900's brick walls.

Special Features:
Two-tone cabinetry, commercial Pro Style cooktop with stainless chimney type hood, built in Sub-Zero refrigerator, two-level Avonite countertops, exposed brick walls, 45 degree angles creates plenty of work space and adds shape to this long rectangular area, specially designed cabinet for commercial style bread slicer.

Dimensions:
12 feet by 18 feet

Products Used:
Cabinetry: Wood-Mode; Flooring: Ceramic/Imola; Countertops: Avonite; Sink(s): Elkay; Faucets: Kohler; Dishwasher: Asko; Cooktop: Thermador; Lighting: Task; Refrigerator: Sub-Zero; Oven: Thermador; Microwave: Panasonic; Compactor: Kitchen Aid; Disposal: Franke.

commercial
transformation

This newly redesigned kitchen was part of a complete revnovation to convert a 22' x 44' second floor commercial space with 14' high ceilings into a one bedroom luxury apartment.

This project posed several challenges, and Michael Stockin, CKD and owner of Kuntriset Kitchens & Baths Design Center teamed up with interior designer Michael McCollough to transform this space into a functional living area.

One of the most unique challenges of this redesign was to conceal a commercial bread slicer which weighed 150 lbs. This

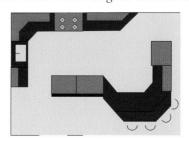

was done by storing the unit out of sight in a specially designed cabinet which enabled it to roll out when needed.

Meeting the homeowner's need for storage and energy efficient products, we looked for products with the ENERGY STAR® label. This means the products meet the ENERGY STAR® guidelines for energy efficiency. A stackable washer and dryer was incorporated into the design, as well as wardrobe cabinets, TV/entertainment cabinets, and a computer desk area. By utilizing these cabinets, the 14' ceiling could run straight through to help enlarge the space. Some of these cabinets were actually hung from the ceiling with rods to provide the quality and appeal of an open and airy look.

These cabinets, in contrast to the exposed brick wall, create a customized kitchen space that makes the best use of this kitchen's unique details. ◆

DESIGNER

Christian O'Donnell
Manzo. Contact
Renaissance Kitchen &
Bath, Inc., 663
Skippack Pike, Blue
Bell, PA 19422;
215/542-5000.

Illusions of space breathe new life into this colonial kitchen's redesign.

timeless
beauty

Special Features:
Custom built hutch, 10 feet by 10 feet back lit pyramid ceiling, synthetic stucco custom framed hood with marble and composite stone tile, Raymond Enkleboll corbels on island, custom built copper top bay window, custom railing, faux painting.

Dimensions:
16.6 feet by 15.6 feet; Nook: 8.9 feet by 6 feet

Products Used:
Cabinetry: Custom-glazed and flyspecked; Flooring: Tagina; Countertops: Granite New Venetian Gold; Sink(s): Franke; Faucets: Kohler; Dishwasher: GE Monogram; Cooktop: GE; Lighting: Halo; Refrigerator: GE Profile; Wallcovering: York; Oven: GE.

The homeowners of this surburban 60 year old stone colonial home dreamed of reinventing their tired and dark kitchen. Low ceilings and the lack of natural light created a dreary room for entertaining, while an inoperable laundry room and enclosed stairwell hindered traffic flow to the beautiful pool and garden area.

The designers at Renaissance Kitchen & Bath worked closely with the home-

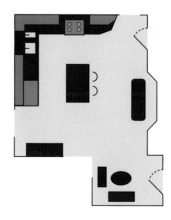

owners to overcome these obstacles while creating an atmosphere of warmth. Walls were removed and a large copper-topped bay window and leaded glass doors were added to allow for the natural flow of light.

To increase the illusion of space, a 10'x 10' pyramid was constructed in the ceiling, complete with cove lighting and faux painting. A custom hutch was added to provide a place to display treasured family heirlooms, as well as providing additional storage.

Custom cabinets finished with a light stain and antique glaze complement the rustic tile floor and granite countertops. Wainscoting and corbels were applied to the island, concealing a convection microwave while allowing counter space for food preparation and casual dining.

The result is a timeless effect that successfully blends lifestyle and ambiance with form and functionality. ◆

This growing family's needs were met by incorporating a large island.

grand new
kitchen

Meeting the needs of a growing family was the primary goal of designer George Kennedy, professional designer with Kennedy Kitchens, in his approach to this grand new kitchen.

The designer accomplished this by including a large center island, capable of seating four, as the focal point of the kitchen. Its unique size and shape enhances the bright open space surrounding it. Bright country blue accents are softened by light maple cabinets, which feature full overlay doors, rolling interior trays, and decorative lighting behind glass doors. Resembling a

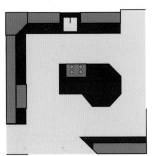

built-in china cabinet, the separate 'hutch' area includes extra-wide drawers for convenient storage of table linens. The generous 47" arched window over the sink lets in plenty of natural light, along with an extraordinary view of the countryside.

Kennedy's careful attention to detail is evident in the many special touches throughout the kitchen – from the staggered heights of the 36" wall cabinets for staging prized collectibles at the top, all the way down to the matching toe kick. The cabinetry which faces the family room is also trimmed to match the cabinets for a complete look.

The final touches in 'Lapis Granite' blue sandwiched around all of the countertop edges, complemented with an accent strip on the deck matching the free-form radius of the massive island, create a customized kitchen masterpiece of unduplicated quality and design. ●

Special Features:
LG Hi-Macs countertops with inlay in deck, wall cabinets 36 and 42 inches high, full overlay doors, decorative drawer fronts, hutch with different heights and depths.

Dimensions:
16.6 feet by 17 feet

Products Used:
Cabinetry: Legacy Division Bertch; Flooring: Bruce Hardwood; Countertops: LG Hi-Macs; Sink(s): LG Hi-Macs; Faucets: Moen; Dishwasher: Kitchen Aid; Cooktop: Jenn-Air; Refrigerator: General Electric; Oven: Jenn-Air; Compactor: Jenn-Air.

DESIGNER

George Kennedy
Kennedy Kitchen
Distributors
2763 S. 6th Street
Springfield, IL 62703
217/793-2284

Photographer: Robin Victor Goetz

A custom made arch over the cooktop creates a unique focal point to this room.

advance
planning

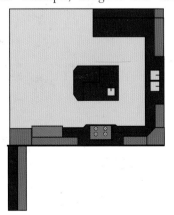

The owners of this spacious new home in a Cincinnati suburb of Montgomery, Ohio started planning their kitchen design one full year in advance. Despite all of the planning, however, this eye-catching project turned out to be greatly different from the original plan.

Patrick Ryan, CKD, co-owner of Kitchen Concepts, designed and constructed the new kitchen by appealing to the homeowner's unique tastes. The owners requested a cooktop area that would set their kitchen apart from all others. "We originally were planning to put the cooktop in the corner, but it just didn't work out, so we ended up putting it where it is now, in the center under a custom archway, while decorating it in two different colors of cherry."

Granite tiles on the walls, a custom wine rack to the left of the window, and raised display cabinets on the back side of the peninsula complement the multi-level island. Attention to every detail is evident by incorporating hiding places for pots and pans in deep drawers.

The homeowners now feel that they have the perfect work space in a triangular area that features a refrigerator, commercial stove, and small sink in the island keeping everything in close touch. ◆

Special Features
Arched hood, cooktop, multi-level island.

Dimensions
17 feet by 21 feet

Products Used
Cabinetry: Cabinets by Nichols, Inc.; Flooring: Italian Limestone; Countertops: Uba Tuba Granite; Sink(s): Elkay; Faucets: Gerber, Opella; Dishwasher: Asko; Cooktop: Thermador; Lighting: Corbett, Forecast; Refrigerator: Sub-Zero; Other: Hand painted herbal tiles on backsplash; Wallcovering: File splash-tumble marble, Inside hood, 6 inch granite in absolute black.

DESIGNER

Patrick H. Ryan
is a designer with
Kitchen Concepts, Inc.
Contact the designer
at Kitchen Concepts,
Inc., 6026 Ridge Road,
Cincinnati, OH 45213;
513/531-3838.

Kitchen windows and doors open onto terraces.

Special Features:
Multi-level island; Granite shelf under cabinets for display; custom arched valance

Dimensions:
25' X 23'

Products Used:
Cabinetry: Corsi
Flooring: Wood
Countertops: Granite – Tropic Brown
Dishwasher: Bosch & Fisher Paykel
Cooktop: Thermador
Refrigerator: Sub-Zero

european
panache

The new Italianate home is on the crest of a mountaintop, with a commanding view of beautiful gardens and the Smokey Mountains. No commonplace kitchen could possibly fit into this scenic wonder.

The location, along with the homeowners' love of cooking and family, supplied the inspiration for the design of this home and its French-influenced kitchen. The challenge for Jacque Kitts, of Kitchen Gallery, was to create a warm inviting feeling within the large kitchen space.

The clients wanted generous-sized appliances and expansive cabinetry. They realized that combining many work centers with entertainment areas would allow them to enjoy preparing meals while easily sharing conversation with friends and family.

These goals were met by careful attention to personalized details that would add character to these areas and reflect the uniqueness of this family. A custom-designed hood and soffit minimize the vast plane of the ceiling line and adds a coziness to the kitchen area. The multi-level island not only identifies work areas but also provides a perfect showcase for colorful displays on countertops or in custom-designed niches at its base. The arched valance over the window was designed to mirror its frame so the view can be enjoyed by family and guests.

With the wrap-around bar at one end of the kitchen and the sitting area at the other, movement is easy and allows for many people to gather in comfort—another request of the homeowners. Kitchen windows and doors open onto terraces with fountains, blurring the line between indoors and the breathtaking landscape.

Lighting placement was of utmost importance. It highlights task areas, emphasizes special-interest areas and creates moods.

The finished space beckons visitors to enter into this center of activity that is loaded with panache and charm. It's a perfect gathering place for parties in the evening or for the family to sit in the glow of a mountaintop sunrise for their first cup of morning coffee.◆

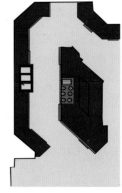

DESIGNER

Rochelle Kalisch
Regency Kitchens
Inc.
4204 14th Avenue
Brooklyn, NY 11219
718.435.4266
And
204 E. St.,1E
New York, NY 10021
212.517.8707

Photographer: Tim Lee

Getting positive vibes in this space was a challenge.

Special Features:

Two column like units effectively separate the kitchen from the rest of the apartment, while retaining the open feeling. A dropped wood ceiling with large square light at the ceiling creates the illusion of a skylight. Quilted stainless steel backsplashes and refrigerator front panels. Stainless steel countertops.

Dimensions:
7' 7" X 8' 7"

Products Used:

Cabinetry: Maple Wood, Regency Kitchens
Flooring: Multicolor granite – International Stone & Accessories
Countertops: Grassi Sheet Metal Works
Sinks: Kindred KSSX2123 S
Faucets: KWC
Dishwasher: Miele
Cooktop: KitchenAid
Lighting: Juno Lights
Refrigerator: Northland

mother-daughter
kitchen

Just like people, every space comes with its own personality and characteristics. Rochelle Kalisch, of Regency Kitchens Inc., has a simple, workable philosophy: Pick out the positive and make it work.

But Kalisch found getting positive vibes in this space was quite a challenge. The kitchen was far from functional. It was small, dark and cramped. Counter space and storage were obviously inadequate.

Standing in the space, she began to visualize a charming and cozy working area, without the separation and closed feeling. Kalisch could relate: She, too, is a working mother. She knows that after a hectic workday, she values the time she can spend with her own children. Interacting with them during the preparation of meals is true quality time: a most enjoyable and enriching cooking experience.

The designer proposed removing the wall between the kitchen and living room and adding an additional counter. This neatly transformed the space into a pleasant and efficiently working kitchen. Counter space is substantially increased, and room for a considerable number of storage cabinets was created. The new counter also doubles as a breakfast bar and homework desk.

The dropped ceiling, maple cabinets, stainless-steel counters and granite flooring all contribute to the drama of the new space.◆

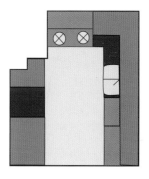

DESIGNER

Jamie Carswell
Total Home Ltd
#81 Reid Street
Hamilton, HM-11
Bermuda
441-296-1366

Photographer: Stephen Raynor

There were many obstructions in the kitchen.

Special Features:
Butcher-block Island; Full height Corian backsplash; original cedar beams; skylight.

Dimensions:
15' x 17'

Products Used:
Cabinetry: Jay Rambo
Flooring: Pembroke Tile & Stone
Countertops: Surface Tech/John Boos – Corian
Sink(s): Whitehaus – Double Equal Stainless Steel 31"
Faucets: Whitehaus-Dolphin pull out spray faucet
Dishwasher: Bosch
Cooktop: Bosch- 36 5 Burner gas cook top-Liquid Propane
Lighting: Tech Lighting/Kichler-Suspended
Refrigerator: Sub-Zero
Vent Hood: Modern Air-36"
Oven: Bosch
Microwave: Sharp – 1.5 cu ft 900 watt combination micro/convection oven
Washer: Frigidaire
Dryer: Frigidaire
Sky Light: Bermuda Glass-Aluminium Framed Window

light
in bermuda

The old Bermuda home needed a new kitchen. The homeowners called upon Jamie Carswell, of Total Home Ltd. as designer. The space was completely gutted, and work began.

The biggest challenge was all the obstructions in the kitchen, which had originally been two rooms with different ceiling heights, divided by 2-foot walls. Four doors, a large window and an electrical panel added to the confusion and left a very restricted space with which to work. The family, while not large, likes to entertain and needed more space.

To gain the feeling of an open room, the ceiling was removed, exposing the original beams of Bermuda cedar. Counteracting the darkness in that section, it was decided to install a skylight in conjunction with the monorail lighting.

The dividing walls were removed and one doorway blocked, resulting in a nice open space. The large window remained to allow as much natural light as possible.

The client wanted to keep the laundry area in the kitchen but needed more working counter space, so front-loading units were chosen, along with a Corian countertop with full backsplash routed to resemble tile. Refrigerator and dishwasher panels smooth out the look and keep it from being too busy.

The island with its unvarnished butcher-block top adds space. Blue with black glaze highlights the crown molding and contrasts nicely with the beams. Because the homeowners wanted a place to store wine and glasses, a wine rack and mullioned glass doors are used between the refrigerator and oven/micro cabinets.◆

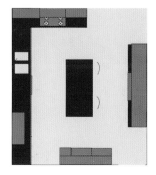

Photographer: George Peirce.com

The owners requested an uncluttered, understated design.

the empty nest
syndrome

When this New Jersey couple decided to relocate nearer their business, they called Andrew Colannino, a Certified Kitchen Designer of Modern Millwork Kitchen & Bath Studio, to design their new kitchen. They wanted a room that was casually elegant, a showcase kitchen for entertaining the family growing with grandchildren, yet intimate enough for dinner for two.

Designing separate areas for the functions they served approached the challenge. A room addition provides a large dining area; double islands accommodate two cooks during family gatherings, yet one single island can be set for two. The homeowners' desire for an uncluttered, understated design is reflected in the champagne on maple custom cabinets with Violetta granite countertops and backsplashes.

The two islands create a galley-type kitchen within the U-shaped design to house sink, refrigerator drawers, double-drawer dishwasher and compactor. The main focus of the cooking area is the six-burner 48-inch range topped with infrared warming shelf and exhaust hood. The owner is an ardent baker, so another 30-inch wall oven topped by a stainless micro-chamber is also included.

A planning desk to store and file recipes completes the area.

A custom tall storage cabinet and secondary sink area flank the refrigerator, completing the U.

Steps away, convenient to the dining room, den and living room, is the 9-foot butler's pantry, replete with glass mullion doors, granite countertop and backsplashes, bar sink, undercounter ice maker and 24-inch wine storage unit.

A showcase kitchen that welcomes grandchildren? These empty-nesters have achieved the best of both worlds. ◆

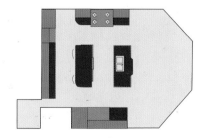

Special Features:
Spacious gourmet design with two islands featuring double drawer dishwasher and under counter refrigerator, drawers.

Dimensions:
18' X 30'

Products Used:
Cabinetry: Champagne on Maple by Lewistown Cabinet Center, Inc.
Countertops: Apex Marble & Granite, Inc.
Sink(s): Kohler
Faucets: Grohe
Dishwasher: Fischer & Paykel
Range: Viking 48" Dual fuel range
Refrigerator: Sub-Zero 48" side x side
Oven: Viking 30" single wall oven w/convection
Other: Sub-Zero wine storage refrigerator; Sub-Zero under counter refrigerator; Broan trash compactor; Scotsman ice-maker

DESIGNER

Andrew Colannino, CKD
Modern Millwork
Kitchen & Bath Studio
624 Washington
Avenue
Belleville, NJ 07109
973-759-5943

DESIGNER

Haskell R. Matheny
Haskell Interiors, LLC.
85 1st Street N.E.
Cleveland, TN 37311
423.472.6409

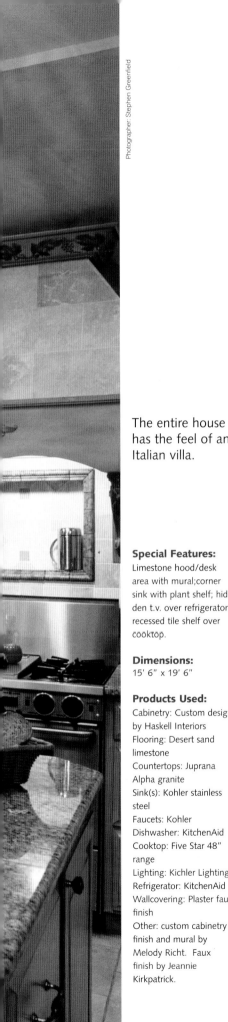

Photographer: Stephen Greenfield

The entire house has the feel of an Italian villa.

tuscany
in tennessee

Special Features:
Limestone hood/desk area with mural; corner sink with plant shelf; hidden t.v. over refrigerator; recessed tile shelf over cooktop.

Dimensions:
15' 6" x 19' 6"

Products Used:
Cabinetry: Custom design by Haskell Interiors
Flooring: Desert sand limestone
Countertops: Juprana Alpha granite
Sink(s): Kohler stainless steel
Faucets: Kohler
Dishwasher: KitchenAid
Cooktop: Five Star 48" range
Lighting: Kichler Lighting
Refrigerator: KitchenAid
Wallcovering: Plaster faux finish
Other: custom cabinetry finish and mural by Melody Richt. Faux finish by Jeannie Kirkpatrick.

This busy professional couple love cooking, entertainment and Italy. They often host large events for local charities and organizations. When they realized it was time to remodel their home of 15 years, they moved out for a year and called upon Haskell Matheny of Haskell Interiors to help with the redesign.

They wanted the feel of an Italian villa, with soft muted colors and relaxed, casual elegance. To that end, Haskell used earth tones, rich stones and metals and aged finishes.

The original kitchen had vibrant bold colors; now the couple wanted a more mature, sophisticated look. They didn't like the cooktop in the island and visualized a new layout with a view of the outdoors, an island with seating and ample work space, a desk area and a television so they could have light meals at the island and keep up with the news. Also requested: a small sitting area for guests to relax in the kitchen and visit while meals are prepared.

This long wish list required tight precision to make every inch count, without adding any square footage. The sink was located under a new corner window; a raised plant shelf allows for growing herbs. With wall cabinetry at a particular premium, an appliance garage was integrated into a cabinet left of the sink to eliminate visual clutter.

Balancing the opposing wall is a refrigerator cabinet and matching pantry, with the desk area in between. For large events, the desk is cleared and used as a work area, with the microwave directly above. A comfortable sofa and tables provide space for guests, and a television set is cleverly hidden above the refrigerator.

As a housewarming gift, the designer commissioned a tile mural of the Italian countryside over the desk area. Now the homeowners and their guests can enjoy their Italian villa with a view (even one that is painted!) while sampling great cooking and fellowship deep in the heart of Tennessee. ◆

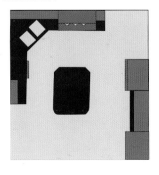

Photographer: Steve Whitsitt

Every wall
in the kitchen
had an opening.

living on
the lake

When this couple decided to build their new home on Canyon Lake in southern California, they envisioned entertaining on the patio and integrating interior and exterior spaces to take advantage of the spectacular view. They wanted to be able to see the lake from the kitchen, dining room and great room. It was important that the kitchen be functional, have large food-preparation surfaces and be easy to clean. They wanted a warm and comfortable environment for a casual dinner for two, yet spacious enough to accommodate large family gatherings.

The greatest challenge was in creating a cozy space when every wall in the kitchen had an opening: from the east, sliding doors to the patio; the north, a passageway to the butler's pantry; west, a passage to the hall; south, a door to the walk-in pantry and a passage to the great room.

Sandra Rodriguez, owner of L&S Interiors, designed a large central island for working and gathering space. It allows for food preparation, serving and seating; traffic flows easily around it from inside to outside. With the cooking and cleaning areas broken up by doorways, the island becomes the wheel from which everything radiates.

The warmth of the soft yellow finish on the cabinets, decorative hood over the cooktop, beadboard on the back of the island, glass doors and careful placement of appliances all add charm to the room. The butler's pantry is a convenient storage and serving area and looks pleasant from both the kitchen and dining room.

The client loves the warm feeling of the kitchen and how well it works when entertaining large or small groups. The granite counters make for easy clean up. And, most importantly, the kitchen has become a natural gathering place. Sitting with guests and enjoying the lake view is like being on vacation. ◆

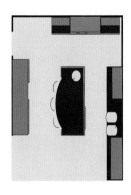

Special Features:
Maize Cabinets
W/Brown Glaze, Custom
Designed Hood, Granite
Countertop, Cross Cut
Travertine Floor,
Adjoining Butler's Pantry
W/Serving Counter,
Walk-In Pantry

Dimensions:
20' X 15'

Products Used:
Cabinetry: Custom
Cabinets by Designer
Flooring: 18" X 18"
Turkish Cross Cut
Travertine
Countertops: Verde
Butterfly Granite
Sink(s): Main & Island
Sink: Kindred Stainless
Steel Undermount
Faucets: Main Sink -
KWC, Island Sink –
Grohe Bar Faucet
Dishwasher: Bosch
Cooktop: Thermador Pro
36" Gas Six Star Burner
Refrigerator: 48" GE
Monogram
Oven: Thermador 30"
Double Oven
Hood: Vent-A-Hood
Custom Liner, Ice
Machine: Scotsman

DESIGNER

Sandra Rodríguez
L & S Interiors
427 South Black Oak Rd.
Anaheim Hills, CA 92807
714.998.8477

DESIGNER

Lee Thomas, CR
Lee Thomas Construction
805 North Main Street
North Canton, Ohio 44720
330.494.5455

Photographer: Steve Whittsett

Two cooks are sometimes working simultaneously.

Special Features:
Elevated bartop & dishwasher.

Dimensions:
27' x 15'

Products Used:
Cabinetry: Merit
Flooring: Ceramic
Countertops: Dupont Corian
Sink(s): Dupont Corian - Whitehaus
Faucets: Delta
Dishwasher: KitchenAid
Cooktop: Whirlpool
Lighting: Halo - Seagull
Refrigerator: KitchenAid
Wallcovering: Imperial
Oven: Whirlpool
Other: Pedal Valves

a room
for all reasons

When this Ohio family of four began planning their new home, they knew that the kitchen had to be multi-functional. It was truly to be a room for all reasons, the open center of the home. And it had to tie in visually and stylistically to the rest of the house — especially the adjoining great room and the deck. Their vision was a semiformal look, but yet casual, inviting and warm.

Some of the functions the family envisioned were entertaining, planning and bill-paying and regular family meals.

The homeowners collaborated with Lee Thomas, of Lee Thomas Construction Inc., to make sure their wishes were fulfilled in the most efficient, most attractive, way. Considering the size of the room, budget constraints were relatively tight.

They decided upon ceramic tile flooring, easy-care countertops in DuPont Corian and high-quality appliances. There would be an island with a cooktop, a breakfast bar for quick snacks and meals and an adjoining dining room for larger groups. They wanted the accented painted finish island to have the look of a piece of furniture; granite was chosen for its countertop.

The ell-shaped red-cherry-stained cabinets define the major work area of the space. Crown and dentil molding ties into moldings used in other rooms, while glass doors make good display areas. Because there was no window near the sink, the clients asked for it to be installed to face an exterior door. Although there was not much wall space, Thomas configured a plan that provides optimum placement of appliances and creates an easy traffic flow—especially vital, as two busy cooks are sometimes working simultaneously.

The desk is large, with plenty of space for a computer, office materials and meal planning. A pantry takes care of food storage. Ergonomic considerations were also planned for; there are pedal valves at the sink, and the dishwasher is elevated for ease. The height of the bartop was also carefully calculated for the best use by members of the family.

Everyone is pleased with the final results, and the space has already proved to be perfect for the smallest breakfast, the biggest party. ◆

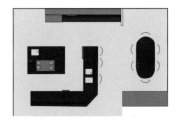

DESIGNER

Don Dinovi, CKD
Kuche + Cucina
489 Rt 17 South
Paramus, NJ 07652
201-261-5221

Photographer: Mark Cunningham

The custom hood shows off a grand collection.

bricks
and beams

Special Features:
Custom Hood with display of owner's collection of hot sauce bottles. Desk/planning center. Hand painted tile mural appliqué. Three piece crown molding. Hand turned posts. Pot rack. Dish display rack.

Dimensions:
15' x 20'

Products Used:
Cabinetry: Kuche + Cucina custom cabinetry.
Flooring: Stained oak hardwood
Countertops: Granite
Sink(s): Franke stainless steel undermount
Faucets: Rohl
Dishwasher: KitchenAid
Cooktop: Thermador/downdraft
Lighting: Litolear recessed ceiling lights and fluorescent under cabinet
Refrigerator: Sub-Zero
Wallcovering: Paint/brick
Oven: Thermador

When these New Jersey homeowners decided to remodel their kitchen, they called in Don DiNovi of Kuche + Cucina to coordinate the process. They carefully calculated the existing elements with their wish list of new features to arrive at the perfect blend of beauty and functionality.

Two walls were brickwork. These would remain, and new elements would be chosen to complement them. One off-center beam would stay in place, and the challenge of integrating it into the whole was met by adding additional beams for a more consistent treatment for the ceiling.

The homeowners are a young family with school-aged children. Naturally, the kitchen becomes a gathering place for more than meals, and they wanted several features to accommodate everyday family life. Among these were a large island that could serve for food preparation, buffet dining and a work center for the children's schoolwork and play-time activities. The grown-ups needed their work center, too, with a desk and a planning area.

Unique to this project was a desire for a display area for the couple's collection of hot sauce bottles. What better place to show these objects than the kitchen? The question was where best to place them. After considering several options,

DiNovi hit upon the creative space of the custom hood.

The island is centered in the kitchen, topped with granite and overhung with a pot rack, which gives a cozy, working-kitchen feel and puts these often-used items within easy reach. Because the family loves to gather informally, the island is a popular place.

Custom cabinetry in cherry wood with a red-hot glaze warms the area even on the coldest days. Stained oak flooring contributes to the cozy feeling and complements the brick and painted wall surfaces. Three-piece crown molding adds importance to the overall look without appearing stuffy or formal.

Now there's no question about the heart of this home. It's the welcoming warmth of the fantastic new kitchen.◆

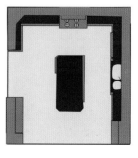

Photographer: Steve Whitsitt

A large
workable
island was very
important.

kitchen
magnificent

A spacious plan, a generous amount of windows and light, a warm and inviting space—these were the desires of the homeowners in visualizing the look of their new kitchen.

Kitchen specialist Sandra R. Soine, Kitchen Gallery of Spring Grove, listened and shared their vision and was able to achieve their aims.

Being working professionals with children in college, a large workable island was very important to this couple. Sliding up a stool, catching a quick snack, cooking in a functional area and "spreading out for entertaining" were all elements the designer and the clients considered in designing the island.

The combination of ginger maple cabinetry brushed with a soft coffee glaze is enhanced with the contrasting colors of the granite countertops. This marriage of materials resulted in a classic dramatic effect.

A desk area opposite the kitchen and with a connecting butler's pantry were designed with the same warm and inviting look that enhances the transition into the formal dining room.

Features that also proved to be important elements in designing the kitchen area television hidden behind pocket doors in the double oven unit, drawers below the rangetop, a recycle bin adjacent to the corner sink and an open shelf cabinet at the island to house the couple's collection of recipe books. By putting the "icing on the cake," the large crown with dentil moulding tops off this kitchen magnificent in grand style.◆

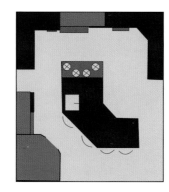

Special Features:
Overall large space; unusually large island area.

Dimensions:
20' x 19' with 20' high ceilings

Products Used:
Cabinetry: Dura Supreme/Valencia Classic Door/Maple-Ginger with Coffee Glaze
Flooring: Ceramic Tile
Countertops: Granite/Yellow Classic with Nordic Green
Sink(s): Blanco/Stainless Steel corner Kitchen Sink/Kohler Veg. Sink
Faucets: KWC
Dishwasher: KitchenAid
Cooktop: Viking
Refrigerator: Viking
Oven: Thermador

DESIGNER

Sandra R. Soine
Kitchen Gallery of
Spring Grove
2404 Spring Ridge
Drive
Spring Grove, IL 60081
815.675.6900
Fax: 815.675.6943

Photographer: Peter Ledwith

Space was a
challenge in
this renovation.

new york
narrows

This project was a complete gut renovation for a single professional woman who travels a lot. When she is at home, however, she likes to cook. As she explained to Guita Behbin of Dura Maid Industries, she wanted all the appliances, storage and counter space that one would expect in a much larger space.

The main challenge was to provide sufficiently wide aisles. Behbin solved that by putting the cooktop modules side by side on an 18-inch counter, placing a single oven/broiler in a tall cabinet and installing an undercounter microwave. This type of arrangement is rarely possible in typical New York City galley kitchens.

The plumbing was modified to allow for a wall-mount faucet and even a deep farmhouse sink. Base and wall cabinets vary in depth for aesthetic and practical reasons. The angles that resulted are accentuated by the floor tile border. Somehow Behbin found enough space for a 36-inch side-by-side refrigerator and a café-style two-person eating area. Further magic touches are evident in the large floor tiles that

create the illusion of more floor space than is actually present.

Color links all the elements, with a light stain on cherry wood and dark green painted accent shelving, trim and moldings. The continuation of crown and baseboard molding throughout the room also pulls it together and creates visual interest.

A narrow space with wide possibilities is the result of what seemed an almost impossible challenge. Now the client enjoys a kitchen that is extremely functional, aesthetically well balanced and very cozy. ◆

Special Features:
light stained cherry
cabinet doors with dark
green. Painted accents
16 X 16 diagonally set
slate floor tiles, farm-
house sink and wall
mount faucet.

Dimensions:
17'6" x 6' 8"

Products Used:
Cabinetry: Jay Rambo
Sink(s): Franke's Manor
House Sink
Faucets: Whitehaus
Collection, Tiffany style
Cooktop: GE Monogram
Lighting: Task undercabi-
net, Luche series
Refrigerator: Sub-Zero
Oven: GE
Microwave: GE

DESIGNER

Guita Behbin
Dura Maid
Industries, Inc.
130 Madison Ave.
New York, NY
10016
212.686.0246

Photographer: Mark Cunningham

A small
space blends
minimalism
with comfort.

crisp
and clean

The new home is a summer house in Pennsylvania, and the homeowner is an architect. No surprise, then, that he was involved in every step of design and construction.

When Bennie Thompson began thinking about the design of his new kitchen, he called in Chaim Sharon of Kuche + Cucina to collaborate and guide the process from idea to completion.

The kitchen area is relatively small (17 by 18 feet), and its ceilings are high. The angled walls are architecturally stimulating but were challenging at times as the designer worked for the ultimate in placement of cabinetry and appliances, ease of traffic flow and the creation of a comfortable and even cozy room with elements of minimalism.

The cabinetry (from SieMatic) was chosen for its sleek lines and minimalist (no hardware) look. Softening that effect is the Anegre wood, with its warm color and its overall effect of quiet elegance. Black granite countertops link the contemporary lines and the warmth of the wood.

Brass, too, takes its place in the mixture, as the designer chose to suspend overboards from

the ceiling with brass rods and to use brass to support the bar-height countertop over the island. Illumination is installed in the overboards.

The island's bi-level counter adds visual interest as well as providing varied surfaces for food preparation and serving, along with display areas for accent pieces. Under all, chestnut-colored ceramic tile flooring contributes to the brilliant blend of contemporary and comfort, ease of use and stunning good looks.

Surprises abound in the newly designed kitchen, but it's no surprise that the homeowner is an architect. His touches are evident everywhere. ◆

Special Features:
Bi-Level counter on island; suspended from ceiling overboard; c channel door style (no knobs or pulls).

Dimensions:
17' x 18'

Products Used:
Cabinetry: SL 505 door by SieMatic
Flooring: ceramic tiles by Dal. Style; stone haven color; chestnut.
Countertops: granite; black absolute
Sink(s): Franke
Faucets: Franke
Dishwasher: Miele
Cooktop: Dacor Downdraft
Lighting: Low voltage halogen fixtures
Refrigerator: Sub-Zero 650
Wallcovering: Granite backsplash
Oven: Dacor
Warming drawer: Dacor

DESIGNER

Chaim Sharon
Kuche & Cucina
489 Rt. 17 South
Paramus, NJ 07652
201.261.5221

Photographer: Ray McCoy

The cabinetry
will grow
richer with
the patina of
wear.

library
look

The totally remodeled kitchen designed by Kelly Zamonski, of The Kitchen Place, Inc., is as sophisticated as the rest of this art collector's home. It exudes the warmth and comfort of an estate library and is a retreat rather than a stage, a place for quiet intimacy and reflection rather than a lavish entertainment space.

Zamonski created the custom cherry raised-panel cabinetry with an arched valance and columned pilasters to grow richer with the patina of wear. The owners welcomed the floor-to-ceiling inset cabinets for the extra storage, and the full-length illuminated glass corner cupboards perfectly display their art glass collection. An abundance of large and small drawers invite adventures of discovery. Rich dark countertops complete the overall atmosphere of luxury.

Reflecting the owner's collection of oriental rugs, ceramic tiles were inset into the concentric narrow plank red oak floor. The resulting kitchen "rug" is not only attractive but provides a tough, easy-to-clean surface.

The friendly, open square kitchen offers four comfortable workstations and a clever pigeonhole message center. It's easy to access the refrigerator and large pantry without even entering the work spaces. A bi-level peninsula shields the cooktop from the adjoining seating area while allowing the cook (or cooks) to converse easily with guests. Above the cooktop hangs a copper hood like a floating sculpture, uniting all the elements of this unique kitchen into a single work of art.◆

Special features:

Multi-level granite counters, floor to ceiling cabinetry, custom arched valance, with columned pilasters down to counter. inset door style, message center, ceramic tile inset into concentric wood floors gives appearance of area rug.

Dimensions:
12' x 12.5'

Products Used:

Cabinetry: DutchMaid Custom Kitchens
Flooring: Narrow plank red oak
Countertops: Granite-Dakota Mahogany
Dishwasher: ASKO
Cooktop: Dacor
Wallcovering: Paint

DESIGNER

Kelly Zamonski
The Kitchen Place,
Inc.
1163 West Second
Street
Xenia, OH 45385
937.372.6959

This kitchen design captured the grand ocean views of this luxurious vacation home.

spacious entertaining
carefree style

This spacious island vacation home in Wilmington, North Carolina has been known to entertain several generations of people at one time with its view of endless miles of ocean, inviting a carefree and never ending locale for good times.

Cynthia Sporre, CKD and owner of Kitchen Blueprints, was asked by interior designer Tina Williamson, ASID, to create a grand yet intimate kitchen space that

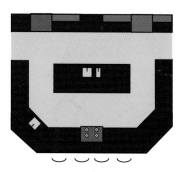

could accommodate multiple families at once, while retaining a comfortable atmosphere for vacationing and socializing.

The designer accomplished this by selecting a recessed maple door style for the cabinetry, which highlights just a touch of the soft 'heirloom' white glaze. The Corian tops with sleek edge and gentle flecking reminisce of the sandy stretches of beach outside. The kitchen layout incorporates horizontal surface areas, two islands, and a second vegetable sink making the space comfortable for several helpers. Matching appliance panels and a view of the coordinating living room minimize an atmosphere of "work".

Attention to both space and atmosphere in the grand design successfully provided the kitchen with all of the fun, comfort and freedom of their luxurious vacation home…view included. ●

Special Features:
Long bar to seat eight people, two islands, airy space with ocean view, view of coordinated entertainment center, double appliance garages, custom appliance panels, vegetable sink.

Dimensions:
19.6 feet by 17 feet

Products Used:
Cabinetry: Wood-Mode "Hallmark II"; Flooring: Maple Wood; Countertops: Corian "Everest"; Sink(s): Kohler undermount; Faucets: Moen single control; Dishwasher: Kitchen Aid; Cooktop: Kitchen Aid; Refrigerator: Sub-Zero; Oven: Thermador.

DESIGNER

Cynthia Sporre, CKD.
Contact Kitchen
Blueprints Inc., 4231-D
Princess Place Dr.,
Wilmington, NC
28405; 910/763-2536.

DESIGNER

Beusha Pelkey,
Contact Kitchen
Concepts, 210 Daniel
Webster Hwy.,
Nashua, NH 03060;
603/891-2600.

Minimal available space was maximized by utilizing every nook and cranny.

new england
ambiance

Special Features:
Multi level counter on island, granite tops, custom bookshelf at end of island, recessed sink and cooktop cabinets.

Dimensions:
13 feet by 23 feet

Products Used:
Cabinetry: Kountry Kraft stained maple with matching wood knobs; Flooring: Natural Oak Wood; Countertops: Juperano Columbo Granite; Sink(s): Kindrid Stainless Steel Undermount; Faucets: Grohe Ladylux; Dishwasher: Bosch; Cooktop: General Electric; Lighting: Hubberton Forge and Tiffany; Refrigerator: General Electric; Wallcovering: Paint; Oven: General Electric; Furniture: Nicholas & Stone.

This professional couple decided to build their new home in beautiful and majestic Windham, New Hampshire, setting the stage for a kitchen designed to capture New England style. Beusha Pelkey, professional designer with Kitchen Concepts, was selected to create a kitchen that would complement the rest of this engaging new home.

Due to the location of a door leading to the deck, as well as an opening to the living room and a doorway into the dining room, there was little available space to

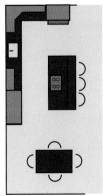

design the type of kitchen the homeowners dreamed of. The designer made the most out of the available space by utilizing the large opening to the living room to house a multi-level island. This location keeps the General Electric cooktop out of reach of small children, while additionally hiding kitchen clutter from the adjacent living room.

The recessed fronts of the sink and cooktop cabinets, as well as the decorative open shelf cabinet, creates a welcoming entrance leading from the dining room into the kitchen. To create a comfortable and relaxed feeling, Kountry Kraft cabinetry in stained maple was used. The beaded inset and Shaker doors with matching wood knobs complete the homeowners' desired look. The specially designed appliance garage and pantry keeps everything neatly in place, and the Juperano Columbo granite countertops, featuring an 18 inch backsplash, provides the ideal finishing touch to a kitchen designed with the homeowners' primary needs in mind. ●

Photographer: J. Miles Wolf

Short on wall space, the butler's pantry became a "back-up" kitchen.

1920's
tudor style

Before considering uprooting their family to Cincinnati, the homeowners of this 1920's tudor-style home had a long list of goals that needed to be attended to. They selected Architects Plus and John Daniman Carpentry, Inc., make their dreams come true.

Once Kirk Hodulik of Architects Plus designed the great room/kitchen addition,

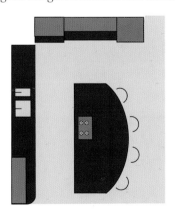

the homeowners turned to Bzak Design Group to design the kitchen/butlery that would make the transition to their new home an easy one. Since the kitchen was short on wall space, the butlery became a "back-up" kitchen housing a second refrigerator, freezer, sink and dishwasher.

The pantry and wall cabinet storage adequately stores the owners' collections of dinnerware for every occasion, and a corner wine-rack keeps an ample supply of wine on hand for entertaining.

The plate-rack hutch furniture cabinetry became the kitchen's focal point, complemented by the hand-painted island countertop. With the selection of warm wood tones and "aged" finishes on the cabinets, beams and floor, a sense of a lived-in look blends seamlessly with the new addition to make it look as though it were an original. ◆

Special Features:
Butlery used to be original kitchen area, beamed ceiling, accent plate-rack hutch cabinetry, hand-painted tile island and backsplash, hot-water heated floor.

Dimensions:
Kitchen: 15 feet by 21 feet; Butlery: 11 feet by 24 feet

Products Used:
Cabinetry: Custom; Flooring: Distressed Pine heated by a hot water system; Countertops: Corian and hand-painted tile; Sink(s): Kohler; Faucets: Concinnity; Dishwasher: Asko and Kitchen Aid; Cooktop: Thermador; Refrigerator: Sub-Zero; Oven: Thermador.

DESIGNER

Karen A. Bieszczak,
CKD. Contact Bzak
Design Group, 5101
Creek Rd., Cincinnati,
OH 45242;
513/984-9445

DESIGNER

Don DiNovi, CKD
Kuche + Cucina
489 Rt. 17 S.
Paramus, NJ 07652
201.261.5221

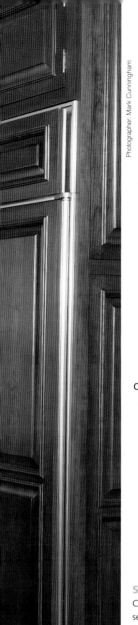

Photographer: Mark Cunningham

Glass-front cabinetry allows treasured items to become decorative accents.

magnificent
in manhattan

Special Features:

Custom hood; window seat; island bookcase; four-piece crown molding; detail carpentry such as reeded corners, rosettes and door with molding application; hardwood flooring; granite countertops; recessed ceiling lights

Dimensions:

12' 6" x 16'

Products Used:

Cabinetry: Kuche + Cucina
Sink: Rohl
Faucets: Rohl
Dishwasher: Miele Incognito
Refrigerator: Sub-Zero

Space is always a watchword in kitchen design, whether it's a remodel or a new construction. Space in New York City, however, is at a real premium. When the owners of this Manhattan apartment decided to remodel their kitchen, that magic word was high on their list. But they wanted more. Their apartment overlooks the Hudson River, and they realized it was possible to allow a view of the river from their new kitchen.

Turning to a professional designer, they outlined their situation and expressed their dreams, which included a full-size traditional home-style kitchen. The homeowners decided to gut the space to allow Don DiNovi flexibility in design

Storage needs were addressed with custom cabinetry. Details abound, including hand-turned reeded columns and molding. A tall pantry takes advantage of vertical space, building up rather than out. But it does more than hold the necessities. It also camouflages unsightly

mechanical features. As DiNovi explains, "Since we could not move the pipes, we hid them."

Professional appliances, a custom-built range hood with recirculating blower, and a handy island ensure years of comfort and ease of use as the homeowners, a professional couple, relax and entertain guests. Best of all, the luxurious apartment now affords a beautiful view of the river from the work space. ◆

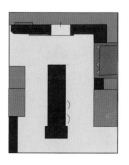

DESIGNER

Christian Manzo
Renaissance
663 Skippack Pike
Blue Bell, PA 19422
215.542.5000

Photographer: John Martinelli

The island houses a downdraft stove and a microwave.

from conventional
to conversational

Special Features:
Multi-level island with downdraft stove and undercounter microwave; 12-foot radial window; structural columns covered in coral stone; AC ducts and plumbing disguised in multiple piece crown and chases in cabinetry; corbels and wrap-around fluting on island; faux-finished walls; custom cabinets

Dimensions:
16' x 32'

Products Used:
Flooring: Tagina ceramic tile
Countertops: Zodiac
Backsplash: Aster from Italy
Sink(s): Corian
Faucets: Kohler
Dishwasher: KitchenAid
Stove: Thermador
Lighting: Kichler, Seagull
Refrigerator: KitchenAid
Hardware: Top Knobs

The owners of this traditional colonial home needed to reinvent their U-shaped kitchen to add light and redefine traffic patterns.

The new design boasts a 12-foot-high radial window, flooding the rooms with much needed light. An addition that enlarged the family room adds a casual, yet elegant eating area, plus space for an island and desk. Seeded-glass lighting, tiled flooring, textured columns, glazed cabinetry and design accents create a relaxed feel with European flair.

A faux finish on mocha-colored walls complements the caramel glazed cabinetry. Coral stone columns built into the desk area define and create a natural divide into the new great room and also house structural posts. Quartz countertops and black wrought iron accents, including light fixtures, cabinetry hardware and stools, create drama and balance. Undercabinet lighting showcases a tumbled marble backsplash. The 7-foot island houses a downdraft stove, eliminating the need for an overhead hood, the microwave, which provides wall space for a decorative dish rack and a seeded glass door cabinet. Fluted columns and corbels finish the multi-level island.

Existing mechanicals are hidden with custom pantry cabinets and a three-piece crown. The refrigerator, dishwasher and trash compactor are paneled to provide a seamless flow of cabinetry. Finishing touches include a variety of accessories that add charm and texture.◆

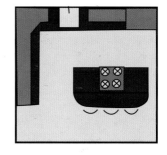

DESIGNER

Susan Lund
Spacial Design
2 Penny Lane
Fairfax, CA 94930
415.457.3195

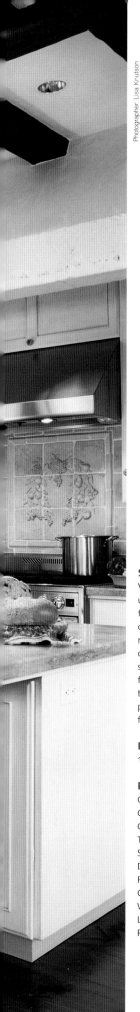

Photographer: Lisa Knutson

Natural stone counters and white pine flooring keep this kitchen down to earth.

reborn
beauty

Special Features:
Void space in sink wall used to create a custom flip-up door to conceal countertop appliances; root storage drawers; custom, concrete backsplash tiles; diamond-finish, integral-color, two-coat appliance plaster; white pine flooring

Dimensions:
17' x 24'

Products Used:
Cabinetry: Custom Cabinetry
Countertops: Honed Travertine
Sink(s): Blanco
Dishwashers: Bosch
Range: Dynasty
Oven: Viking
Warming Drawer: Viking
Lighting: Halo
Refrigerator: Viking

Breathtaking views of San Francisco Bay command attention in this house constructed on a lot where the owner's previous home, destroyed by a winter storm, once stood. The new home's design is reminiscent of a Tuscan villa with its rich, textured plaster walls and hand-hewn beams with dovetail connections. The earthiness of concrete tile backsplashes and honed Travertine counters is complemented by glazed-finish cabinets embellished with hand-painted ceramic knobs imported from Italy.

The wall oven is the workhorse of the kitchen. It is mounted at waist height; a warming drawer is located below. Other appliances are stainless steel, for a clean, professional look.

Susan Lund's challenge was to design a practical and efficient workspace for effortless entertaining and meal preparation. The homeowners wanted two dishwashers, a walk-in pantry, recycling center and an oversized appliance garage. In addition, they wanted space for their three young children to play and complete homework and other projects nearby but outside the main work triangle.

A large L-shaped, multifunctional island with prep sink and chopping block provides several areas for two cooks to work simultaneously, as well as space for guests to visit with the cooks. Adjacent to the kitchen is a breakfast nook and desk area for menu planning, list making or surfing the Internet.

With plenty of space for the entire family, the newly remodeled kitchen is both functional and fabulous, and is a main hub of activity.◆

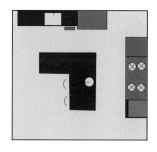

DESIGNER

Pauline Walsh
Schotanus
Construction, Kitchen
& Bath Division
308 Providence Road
Grafton, MA 01590
508.234.7236

Trim work is natural maple with a cherry strip.

arts & crafts
showcase

Special Features:
Character cherry wood/ black accents; glaze and distressing finish; furniture-style cabinetry; multi-level countertop; built-in hutch and eating area; gourmet appliances; wood grid doors

Dimensions:
22' x 18'
plus 15' x 9' eating area

Products Used:
Cabinetry: Plato Woodworking
Flooring: Hardwood
Countertops: Tri-State Stone, Verdi Butterfly Gold granite; natural cherry wood on hutch and desk
Sinks: Franke
Faucets: Rohl
Dishwasher: Asko
Cooktop: Dacor
Lighting: Hubbardton Forge Fixtures
Refrigerators: Sub-Zero
Ovens: Dacor
Hood: Plato
Microwave: GE

The homeowners, both doctors, dreamed of a new home with an old arts and crafts feel and an open floor plan. So they contacted builder Pete Schotanus, who enlisted the design expertise of Pauline Walsh. He gave her carte blanche to create a fabulous, functional kitchen with gourmet flair and a traffic-friendly layout for the busy family of six.

To facilitate traffic, a raised, granite-top bar acts as a divider, defining the cook's space and the family space. To facilitate function, the bar incorporates a 25-inch-deep tabletop. Walsh created storage near the sink and used two 4-inch chamfer posts, pulled forward, for depth.

Professional-grade appliances, such as two Sub-Zero refrigerators and Dacor's stainless steel cooktop, which has copper accents, not only serve the needs of the homeowners, they add to the arts and crafts feel of the room.

Although the room is spacious and open, there is minimal wall space. To meet this challenge, Walsh combined the workspace to the left and right of the cooktop with the landing space for the oven and refrigeration units. To balance the room, the weight of the kitchen wall is countered with an eat-in breakfast nook. The spaces are linked with a built-in hutch that flows into a window seat. The hutch includes arts and crafts flair, as do so many other aspects of the kitchen, showcasing the designer's ability to creatively meet the demands of her clients.◆

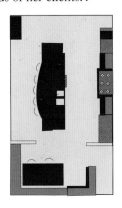

DESIGNER

Suzanne S. Stockford, CKD, is a professional designer with Triangle Design Kitchens, Inc. Contact the designer at Triangle Design Kitchens, 5216 Holly Ridge Drive, Raleigh, NC 27612; 919/787-0256.

Photographer: Jon Zachary

Design interest is captured through the island's use of bun feet to create a 'floating look.'

heightened allure

Special Features

Tiles, recessed niche match arched lighting cornice. Cabinets are of multiple heights and depths.

Dimensions

19 feet by 10 1/2 feet

Products Used

Cabinetry: Plain & Fancy Custom Cabinetry; Flooring: Hardwood, Stained Oak; Countertops: Granite, Ubatuba, Sink: Franke, Faucets: Hansa & Chicago Faucet; Dishwasher: Asko; Cooktop: Dacor; Lighting: Hera; Refrigerator: Sub-Zero; Wallcovering: Paint; Oven: Dacor, Double Ovens.

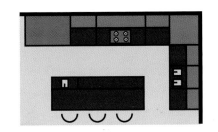

Presented with a kitchen that was poorly designed and inefficient, these homeowners enlisted the professional design services of Suzanne Stockford, of Triangle Design Kitchens, to create a room that was warm and inviting, while blending with the unique collection of antiques that adorned their lovely home.

One of the greatest challenges this designer faced was to create efficient work and storage spaces that would accommodate the difference in heights between the two homeowners. She, barely standing 5 feet tall, had difficulty accessing high storage areas. He, at 6 feet tall, experienced one too many bumps on his head and knees from reaching into low-lying areas. The designer solved this problem by creating work spaces including multiple height and depth cabinetry, extra-deep countertops and wall cabinets in the main work areas, and pantry storage with lots of door racks. Tray storage was also located in the middle rather than at the top of the cabinets to satisfy the shorter of the two.

Other special features include large pull-out drawers with heavy-duty, full-extension drawer guides for easier access to heavy pots and pans, a spice storage, and a tall china storage cabinet beside the desk.

All of these features combine to create an easily accessible and user-friendly kitchen, putting an end to all of those bumps and bruises from too much stretching. Who said you can't get rid of stretch marks? *Ouch!* ◆

Photographer: Mark Rotta

Handcrafted cabinetry and a handpainted tile backsplash transform this kitchen into a custom designed room.

english
charm

The formidable challenge presented to designer Don DiNovi, of Kuche & Cucina, was to transform the existing home's dark 1970s kitchen and dining area into the charm of an English country cottage.

To create a functional kitchen with a dining area for casual weekend family events, DiNovi incorporated an island and peninsula into the plan. This helped to maximize counter surfaces and define workstations, using two-sided glass door cabinetry at the peninsula allowing for ample storage and increased light flow.

A handpainted tile mural blossoms on the backsplash, while polished granite counters add a vibrant expression of the good life. The cabinetry features hand-turned furniture legs, beadboard panels, inset raised panel doors and a custom-built wood hood.

To accommodate the client's love for gourmet cooking, DiNovi selected top-of-the-line appliances including a Viking commercial range, Sub-Zero refrigerator and a Miele dishwasher to surround the convenient work triangle.

This splendid melding of function and design, along with a masterwork of materials, breathed fresh air into an outdated kitchen that this homeowner can once again enjoy. ◆

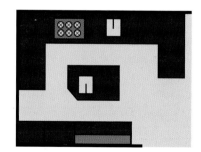

Special Features
Custom wainscot hood. Special paint finish. Handpainted tile splash.

Dimensions
17 feet by 30 feet

Products Used
Cabinetry: Kuche & Cucina; Flooring: Ceramic Tile; Countertops: Granite; Sinks: Frantic Stainless Steel; Faucets: KWC; Dishwasher: Miele; Lighting: Fluorescent Under Cabinet; Refrigerator: Sub-Zero; Wall covering: Wallpaper; Backsplash: Handpainted Ceramic Tile.

DESIGNER

Donald E. DiNovi is a design professional with Kuche & Cucina. Contact the designer at Kuche & Cucina, 489 Rt. 17S, Paramus, NJ 07652; 201/261-5221.

DESIGNER

David M. McNulty,
CKD, is a design
professional with
Kitchen & Bath
Creations, Inc. Contact
the designer at Kitchens
& Bath Creations, Inc.,
604 Devon Ave., Park
Ridge, IL 60068;
847/696-1860.

Photographer: Mike Kaskel

The specially designed wooden hood forms the crowning touch to this elegant kitchen.

european flair

Special Features
Double apron sink. Plumbing fixtures in copper and brass. Tumbled travertine tiles on backsplash. Inverted baseboard molding with dentil crown.

Dimensions
23 feet by 12 feet

Products Used
Cabinetry: Holiday-Elite Series; Flooring: Porcelain Tiles; Countertops: Granite; Sinks: Kohler; Faucets: Herbeau; Dishwasher: Asko; Lighting: Juno Trac 12; Refrigerator: KitchenAid; Wallcovering: Faux Finish Over Textured Plaster; Range: Dynasty; Specialty Faux Finish: Greinhouse Designs.

The owners of this 1930s chalet-style home wanted to introduce new cabinetry and materials into their kitchen that would complement the home's French country architecture.

David McNulty, CKD, of Kitchen and Bath Creations, Inc., took on this challenge by first selecting a rich hickory wood with flat recessed panels adorned with a warm golden stain for the new cabinetry. The apron sink and Herbeaux faucet successfully bring the European theme to life.

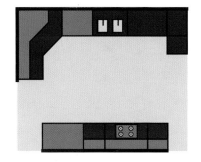

McNulty's biggest challenge was to remove the wall separating the dining area and the mud room, as well as to provide height to the boxed-in ceiling. The ceiling line was covered in a decorative acanthus crown molding with an additional chair rail to give the walls a capped appearance.

Carefully selected tumbled travertine tiles with a pattern design is accented by the recessed niche above the range. The walls were plastered with a textured finish and faux painted to provide that Old World, European feeling. Possessing a flair for gourmet cooking, high-quality appliances were selected including a 36-inch commercial-style range, and a 42-inch refrigerator, which was mandatory for this hungry family of five.

Porcelain tile flooring adds a finishing touch of texture and strength to this new design, making a beautiful transition as this Old World kitchen arrives in the New World. ◆

DESIGNER

Don Boico is a design
professional and
Owner of Classic
Kitchen & Bath Center.
Contact the designer
at Classic Kitchen &
Bath Center, 1062
Northern Blvd.,
Roslyn, NY 11576;
516/621-7700.

Photographer: Peter Ledwith

The beaded inset cabinet doors create an authentic country charm.

restored and
renewed

Special Features
Beaded inset cabinet doors. Angled island counter providing seating and work space. Pantry adjacent to range houses microwave.

Dimensions
18 feet by 13 feet

Products Used
Cabinetry: Craftmaid; Counters: Granite/Ceramic Tile; Dishwasher: Bosch; Refrigerator: Sub-Zero; Range: Garland; Sink: Franke; Faucets: Franke; Lighting: Halo.

The tragedy of a fire led to the creation of this completely remodeled kitchen in Roslyn, New York. Among the homeowners' requests was a more open space, an authentic country look, and functionality of design to suit the wife's love for cooking.

Professional designer Don Boico, of Classic Kitchens & Baths, started out by removing the fire- and water-damaged walls, including a load bearing wall. With over 200 square feet now available, Boico went to work to fill the rest of his client's wishes.

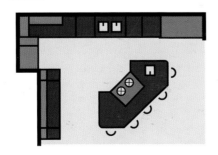

The large center island with a vegetable sink now provides adequate work space for the cook and her helpers. An existing five-foot Garland range was refurbished, continuing to provide commercial-quality cooking and superb baking power. The range, together with a four-foot Sub-Zero refrigerator and ample counter space, all help to transform this kitchen space into a meal-prep paradise.

Special treatments on the cabinet doors, including cut nails, recessed wood pegs and antique markings add to its authenticity. A thorough feeling of warmth is achieved through the crown detail molding on the wall cabinets, contrasting with the antique green island and farm-style brass fixture. All of these details, along with the carefully selected cabinets with beaded inset doors and a spice finish, set the final stage for the "country" look these homeowners desired. ◆

DESIGNER

Nick G. Virgilio, CKD, CGR
Janco Design Group, Inc.
236 Crest Court
Bloomingdale, IL 60108
630.529.2487

Photographer: Mike Kaskell, Kaskell Photography

The interesting shape of the island's granite top nearly doubled the existing counter space.

exquisitely
efficient

Special Features:
Custom tile design on floor and backsplash, decorative plate insert on wall between range and hood, generous storage and counter space.

Dimensions:
21' x 17'

Products Used:
Cabinetry: Merit
Door: Whistler Wood,Cherry
Flooring: CDC Tile
Countertops: Granite—Tropical Brown
Sink(s): Moen
Faucets: Whitehaus
Dishwasher: Bosch
Range: FiveStar
Lighting: Tresco
Refrigerator: GE Profile
Oven: Thermador Triple Oven
Range hood: Sirius Range Hoods
Soap dispenser: Whitehaus
Hardware: Top Knobs

The challenge presented to Nick G. Virgilio, CKD, CGR, president and owner of Janco Design Group, Inc., was to convert an inefficient pantry into additional storage and counter space in this suburban Chicago home.

The pantry wall to be removed was load bearing with several mechanical items above it, creating a challenge for the structural engineer. They solved this problem by installing two short steel beams flush into the ceiling, allowing the new prairie style cherry cabinetry to occupy that additional space. The cabinets are accented by striking tropical brown granite that was beautifully incorporated into both the ceramic tile backsplash and the ceramic tile floor to complete a custom design created by the homeowner herself.

The focal point of this magnificent kitchen is the cooking center. The commercial style stainless steel FiveStar range is topped by a stainless steel Sirius Range Hood, with a gorgeous ceramic decorative plate inserted into the ceramic tile backsplash between the two appliances.

The island size was increased dramatically, creating space for additional storage as well as a beverage cooler. The interesting shape of the granite top nearly doubled the existing counter space and allowed for a dining and snack area for the homeowners' family.

Emphasizing the spectacular garden view from their kitchen was also a priority. The lush garden was brought indoors by the oversized windows above the sink and the sliding French door overlooking the small pond and brick patio. The finished product is a kitchen with plentiful storage and a place for the whole family to convene and enjoy the comforts of home.◆

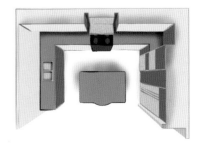

DESIGNER

Sue Rummel is a
Certified Kitchen
Designer with Creative
Solutions Inc. Contact
the designer at
Creative Solutions
Inc., 1471 Danville
Blvd., Alamo, CA
94507, 925/855-9776.

Ample counterspace allows these homeowners to enjoy an efficient workspace with room for lots of entertaining.

casual
formality

Special Features
Two-toned cabinetry.
Efficient work triangle.
Generous island for prep
and casual entertaining.
Separate clean up zone
with trash compactor
and recycle bins

Dimensions
18 feet by 18 feet

Products Used
Cabinetry: Jay Rambo
Island and all other
Custom Cabinetry by
S&S Woodworking;
Flooring: Existing
Hardwood; Countertops:
on Island Granite
Juparana Classico and
Corian; Sinks: Franke at
Island and Integrated
Corian; Faucets: Hansa,
Chicago, Rohl;
Dishwasher: Bosch;
Cooktop: Viking
Professional; Lighting:
Task Lighting;
Refrigerator: GE
Monogram SS Built-In;
Wallcovering: Faux
Painting; Oven: Viking
Professional; Other: U-
Line Wine Captain,
Enclume Hammered
Steel Pot Rack.

The expansive views, spacious rooms and open feeling throughout the house were just a few of the features that attracted the new homeowners to this magnificent home. The kitchen, however, was in need of a major redesign.

The homeowners contacted Susie Rummel, CKD, of Creative Solutions, Inc. to breathe new life into this tired and disfunctional kitchen space, just as she had done for the kitchen in these homeowners' previous house.

Rummel started out by gutting the kitchen, with the exception of the oak parquet floor and the existing garden window, which remained intact at her client's request. Two distinctive areas were then created, providing ample room for this couple to share their love of cooking. The first area, a food preparation space, takes the form of an efficient work triangle with a 42" stainless steel refrigerator, sink, and professional range. The second area, designed for clean-up space, contains an additional sink, dishwasher, trash compactor, and recycle bins.

This newly remodeled kitchen also accommodates the homeowner's need for plenty of counterspace for both the buffet style and formal entertaining they frequently do. Providing an abundance of counter space, while keeping the warm and intimate feeling that exists throughout the home, the kitchen was designed with a large island of burnished cream cabinetry, topped with a Juperano Classico granite that literally "sparkles" when the sun filters through the garden window.

In the end, the designer was able to meet her client's list of requirements through efficient space planning and carefully selected products…culminating in a culinary masterpiece to be enjoyed whether dining formally, or on casual Fridays. *Jeans permitted!* ◆

For the client who loves to entertain, this kitchen is the perfect room for socializing.

socially
inviting

Specific ideas is what this client had in mind when approaching designer Ellen Shelly to create a kitchen in his new home. Often the host of different size gatherings for family and friends, the owner needed a central gathering place within the kitchen for smaller functions as well as outside of the kitchen for larger events.

Working to meet her client's needs, Ellen began by adding a one level island to allow guests to be close to the preparation area as well as be a part of the festivities. Incorporated into the island was a prep sink carefully situated near the range for

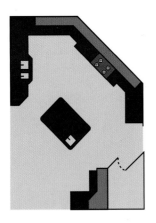

convenience. A walk up two level bar was added behind the main sink area to accommodate an overflow of guests. This feature creates a welcome spot for visitors to mingle while the host cooks or cleans up.

Another creative challenge was to incorporate several trim details within the environment that would give the room a European flair while maintaining a warm cozy feel. This was achieved by adding Ramond Enkeboll crown molding in two sizes. A 6" crown was added to the main cabinets with a 9" molding added to the top of the hood in order to enhance the area while providing massive appeal.

The addition of custom turned legs to the lower bases added a vertical element to offset the horizontal flow of the crown detail. With all of these details decided upon, a warm pine inset cabinet was selected with a brown glaze. This allowed for the finer details to stand out against a slightly softened environment.

Cozy and functional were the key ingredients used to cook up exactly what the client ordered. ◆

Special Features:
One level island, hand painted scene behind range, custom cut granite countertop, custom spindle turned legs.

Dimensions:
18 feet x 23 feet

Products Used:
Cabinetry: Woodmode Flooring: ceramic tile; Countertops: 3cm Granite; Sink: Kohler SS; Faucets: Moen; Dishwasher: Asko; Cooktop: Thermador; Refrigerator: SubZero; Wallcovering: custom painted finish; Oven: Thermador (Range); Other: Raymond Enkeboll molding, custom crafted turned legs.

DESIGNER

Ellen A. Shelly is a professional designer with Shelly Design Inc. Contact the designer at Shelly Design Inc., 1118 Flick Lane, Batavia, OH 45103; 513/752-1606.

The addition of an island provided multi-functionality to this divine kitchen space.

cherry wood abounds

Rebecca White, professional designer with Bouchard-Pierce, was presented with the client's request to remodel and modernize their kitchen, which was not an unusual task for a designer with thirteen years of experience. However, the challenge needed to be tailored around the client's desire to not move any doors, windows, or walls. In addition, the owners wanted to match the wood species and color of the kitchen cabinets to an existing cherry hutch and breakfast nook table. This seemingly simple task quickly took on a more challenging form than an average kitchen update.

The molding was first traced and then sent off to the cabinet manufacturer to ensure that it would be copied exactly.

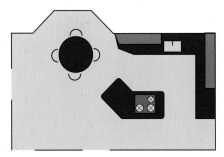

With all of the windows and walls intact, the customer wanted the current arch window to become the focal point of the kitchen. To accomplish this, taller cabinets were used to flank the window and draw attention to the entire area. The arch doors on the wall cabinet continue this theme throughout the kitchen.

The main change came when replacing the U-shaped kitchen with an island design. This addition made way for such appliances as a downdraft range, which also acted as a space saver with a special size drawer to accommodate the client's collection of large pots and pans. Because the back of the island is visible from the living room, custom designed panels were used to draw the eye to the island and back up to the desired focal point of the arched window.

This popular piece has become well-loved by family members and guests who can either dine or mingle at the main attraction. Even the two yellow labs now have room to be close at hand without being underfoot. With several challenges simply conquered this remodeling mission was completed. ◆

Special Features:
Built in refrigerator, island downdraft range, custom designed panels on back of island, pull out base panty, large bottom drawer base in the island.

Dimensions:
10 feet x 12 feet

Products Used:
Cabinetry: Candlelight Natural Cherry; Flooring: Oak; Countertops: Granite — Black Onyx; Sink: Kohler SS Undermount; Faucets: Kohler; Dishwasher: Whirlpool; Refrigerator: GE SXS; Other: Range Jenn-air, Coffeemaker-Black and Decker, Microwave-GE, CD Player-GE

DESIGNER

Rebecca White is a designer for Bouchard-Pierce. Contact the designer at Bouchard-Pierce, 127 Pearl Street, Essex Jct, VT 05452; 802/878-4822

DESIGNER

David McNulty is a
Certified Kitchen
Designer with Kitchen
and Bath Creations,
Inc. Contact the
designer at Kitchen
and Bath Creations,
Inc., 604 Devon
Avenue, Park Ridge, IL
60068; 847/696-1860.

An updated kitchen is tailored to match a home filled with historic features.

Photographer: Mike Kaskel

a perfect
match

Special Features:
Hand carved wood hood, hand crafted ceramic backsplash tile, Brazilian walnut parquet floors, carved multi level island.

Dimensions:
18 1/6 feet X 21 1/3 feet

Products Used:
Cabinetry: Craftmaid; Flooring: Brazilian Walnut Parquet; Countertops: Granite — Santa Cecelia; Sink: Franke and Elkay; Faucet: KWC; Dishwasher: Kitchen Aid and Bosch; Range: Dacor ERSNM8 / Epicure; Refrigerator: SubZero 542 Series; Wallcovering: The Fine Line; Other: warming drawer — Dacor, wine cooler — Marvel.

This historic home situated on Chicago's North Shore area is comprised of Colonial architecture with interiors adorned in Elizabethan elegance and American traditional charm. The intricate details throughout the home demanded that the kitchen maintain the same monochromatic scheme.

Designer David McNulty was hired by these newlyweds to create a kitchen they

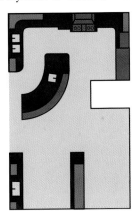

would adore as much as their old world culture home. McNulty achieved this by selecting handmade tiles in a color that would blend the countertops with the hand crafted cabinetry, without distracting the eye. A detailed design pattern at the range was carefully crafted to add depth and richness to this area.

A butler's pantry was incorporated into the design to serve several functions. Safe haven for antique dishware and entertainment goblets, this addition provided room for extra counter space. This expansive preparation place was also welcome by caterers who used it during the couple's wedding reception.

Finally, careful attention to detail prompted McNulty to include a 30" stainless steel sink. This provides the perfect potting and planting location for the blushing bride to pursue her hobby in flowering horticulture. The end result is a perfect match: an updated kitchen with an historic feel. ◆

DESIGNER

George R. Kennedy is the owner and designer of Kennedy Kitchens. Contact the designer at Kennedy Kitchen Distributor, 1212 North Street, Springfield, IL 62704; 217/793-2284.

Distressed cherry cabinets are visually tied together with "stand alone" pieces.

Photographer: Tom Stevens — Photo Resource Center

Special Features:
Blending of woods and textures, stand alone kitchen areas, different style cabinets in different groups (Hosier cabinet for old look).

Dimensions:
14 feet x 14 1/2 feet

Products Used:
Cabinetry: Jay Rambo, Inset Door's, distressed cherry glazed; Flooring: wood, walnut, distressed; Countertops: Avonite; Sinks: Avonite, with Avonite skirt to look like country sink; Faucets: Concinnity, Satin Nickel; Island Kitchen: Kohler K3333; Dishwasher: Bosch with custom wood front panel; Cooktop: Range, Kitchen Aid, drop in smooth top; Lighting: Antique oil lamp; Refrigerator: SubZero with stand alone look; Wallcovering: Schumacher & Co. trim Pierre Deux; Other: T.M. Jenn Aire — Micro in Hosier cabinet behind hide away door. Custom hood apron made from walnut from the farm

old world charm

When this couple built their gracious country home, they looked to George Kennedy to create a warm, distinctive kitchen that not only suited their love of entertaining, but also reflected very personal family ties and traditions. "What we were striving for was the look of fine furnishings," Kennedy emphasized. "The challenge as well as the success of this kitchen is in the unique 'stand alone' pieces that achieve the look of furniture and also blend with the custom cabinetry."

Manufactured by Jay Rambo Company, the distressed cherry cabinets feature inset cabinet doors and drawers, as well as the generous use of custom moldings to main-

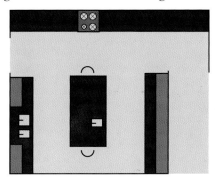

tain a sense of continuity. Details such as bun feet and varied stand alone pieces add to the room's "Old World" charm. Top-of-the-line appliances are attractively integrated with matching wood panels and doors. Of particular interest is the white "Hoosier Cabinet" that opens to reveal ample storage for baking supplies, a convenient work space, and even a microwave oven cleverly concealed in the top section behind hideaway doors.

Working with interior designer Judith Pensoneau-Feurer and the homeowners, Kennedy incorporated crisp country blue and white décor to complement the rich cherry cabinetry. Avonite solid surface countertops were used throughout the kitchen, including a "farmer sink" created by combining an Avonite drop-sink with an Avonite "integral apron" in a second color added to the front.

Finally, strong family connections are tied into the design through the massive walnut board on the range hood made from wood that was brought from the family farm of previous generations, completing this elegant kitchen design. ◆

Country meets Manhattan in this New York City townhouse.

Photographer: Dan Katz

stately elegance in the
big apple

Special Features

Custom Hood. Hand glazed backsplash tile. Island with stainless steel wood edged counter.

Dimensions

15 feet by 32 feet

Products Used

Cabinetry: Kuche + Cucina Handcrafted Cabinetry; Flooring: Handmade Terra Cotta; Countertops: Granite / Stainless Steel Island w/ Wood Trim; Sinks: Kohler - Undermount Cast Iron; Faucets: Moen; Dishwasher: Bosch; Cooktop: Garland Range - Commercial; Lighting: Recessed Ceiling Copper/Brass Island Chandelier; Refrigerator: Trauslan; Wallcovering: Paint; Other: Hand Painted/Glazed Ceramic Tile.

He, a restauranteur, and she, an artist and designer, collaborated with professional designer Don DiNovi, of Kuche + Cucina, for the redesign and planning of this exquisite kitchen remodel in a Manhattan townhouse .

For this large family with four children who entertain often, they envisioned a kitchen that would offer country estate elegance in the heart of New York City.

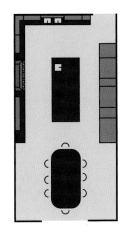

Working from the top down, DiNovi and his client selected a coffered ceiling that extends from the kitchen into the dining area, sporting a custom built glass and wooden ceiling.

Cherry wood cabinetry enhanced with a three piece crown molding detail, brass hinges and hardware surround the light-stained wood island and hood. The custom hood and carved corbels surround a multi-function exhaust system designed to complement the Garland commercial grade range.

Attention to every detail is exemplified in the wood trimmed stainless steel island with chamfered legs and raised side panels, as well as in the backsplash featuring a glazed ceramic tile with fresco-borders. The natural terra cotta flooring is hand-made.

The eclectic selection of furnishings augment the luxurious redesign of this magnificent kitchen space, which is large enough to even have accommodated a fashion show…runway included. ◆

Photographer: Mark Cunningham

The custom booth provides seating for six.

a family-friendly
kitchen

When this young family of four decided to remodel their kitchen, they called upon Certified Kitchen Designer Don DiNovi of Kuche + Cucina for expert help and guidance. Working with the homeowners, DiNovi established the "wish list" and priorities for the floor-to-ceiling remodeling project.

Two work stations were required for food preparation, and because the couple enjoys frequent entertaining, seating was needed for large dinner parties as well as family meals. A further challenge was a steel girder in the ceiling that would have to be concealed.

The designer created a custom booth that not only provides seating for six but includes side compartments perfect for storing the children's toys, coloring books and other items. To hide the girder, DiNovi decided upon a beamed ceiling. This treatment enhances the spacious effect of the room and effectively removes the girder from view.

Now it was time to consider appliances. A built-in refrigerator and professional range were selected, the range highlight-

ed with a custom wood hood. Two sinks were installed, along with 2 dishwashers and work space with microwave. A pot-filler faucet is positioned on the backsplash alongside the range for maximum efficiency.

Hand-cut antique pine flooring installed with peg-face nails along with cherry wood cabinetry add warmth and a feeling of ease and comfort. Walls and ceiling were given a faux-finish treatment, and handpainted tiles were used for the backsplash.

The completed room provides a beautiful, efficient space for family activities and plenty of room to entertain. ◆

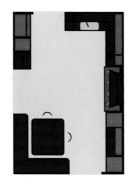

Special Features:
Custom Hood, Hand Painted Tile Backsplash, Pot Filler Faucet, Custom Booth.

Dimensions:
14' X 16'

Products Used:
Cabinetry: Decora
Flooring: Hand cut Pine
Countertops: Granite
Sinks: Franke S/S undermount
Faucets: Rohl
Dishwasher: Miele
Cooktop: Viking
Lighting: Litolear recessed ceiling / Fluorescent under cabinet
Refrigerator: Sub-Zero
Wallcovering: Hand Painted Faux Finish
Oven: Viking

DESIGNER

Don DiNovi, CKD
Kuche + Cucina
489 Route 17 South
Paramus, NJ 07652
(201) 261-5221

DESIGNER

Heidi J. Norcutt
Triangle Design
Kitchens, Inc.
5216 Holly Ridge Drive
Raleigh, NC 27612
919-787-0256

Photographer: Jon Zachary

The spacious '20s kitchen is drenched in natural light.

Special Features:
Juparano Columbo granite island countertop, window seat with drawer storage below, recessed niche in tile backsplash for spice storage

Dimensions:
13'9" X 23'

Products Used:
Cabinetry: Plain & Fancy custom cabinetry
Flooring: American Olean
Countertops: Dupont Corian
Sink(s): Whitehaus Collection farmers sink, Corian bar sink
Faucets: Whitehaus collection
Dishwasher: Asko
Cooktop: Thermador
Lighting: Hera Lighting undercabinet lighting
Refrigerator: Sub-Zero
Oven: Gaggenau
Decorative Hardware: Cal Crystal

a masterful
restoration

Restoring this wonderful 1920s Craftsman-style home to its former glory was the primary goal of these homeowners in Durham, North Carolina. The kitchen remodel was part of a whole-house restoration to undo the damage of years of decline. The house had been divided into apartments, and an unsuccessful kitchen re-do had been attempted by the previous owners. Professional designer Heidi Norcutt and Bill Camp, Certified Kitchen Designer, both of Triangle Design Kitchens, collaborated with Rodney Ward of Rodney H. Ward Design Group to create this spacious new kitchen.

The old kitchen was small and dark, with little room for more than one person to work. The wall between it and the breakfast room was removed to create a large, open space. The team added a big bay window, with a tiled ledge for plants and decorative items, to bring more light into the room. They built a seat below the existing double window for a cozy spot to read and relax. The island is set on simple square legs, giving the feeling of a table, while providing drawers and open slide-out shelves for additional storage. The island is topped with a lively Juparano

Columbo granite counter. An existing butler's pantry was given a fresh coat of paint and new hardware to provide a link to the past amid all the new elements in the kitchen.

The floor is done in a custom ceramic mosaic tile popular in homes built in the early twentieth century. In fact, the 2-inch hexagonal field tiles were produced in the last run of this style and size by American Olean. Of course, extra tiles were ordered should future repairs be needed. The tile continues into the new breakfast room, formerly the back porch.

The professional couple who own this grand old house are delighted with their new spacious kitchen that is drenched in natural light and feels like part of the beautiful outdoors beyond the windows. ◆

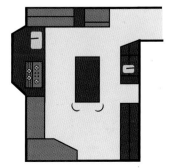

Photographer: John Martinelli

Natural materials add charm to a vacation home.

a bayside
victorian

Expansive views of the Atlantic Ocean and a marina set the mood for an open floor plan in this French-inspired kitchen and great room. The owners of the new home called upon designer Christian Manzo of Renaissance Kitchen & Bath to produce a feeling of casual elegance in their bayside Victorian vacation home. Manzo and the clients worked together to choose the luscious natural materials that contribute so much to the overall effect.

Rich cherry wood is used for the hutch and furniture-styled island, a perfect accent to the surrounding vanilla antiqued and distressed cabinetry. This combination is complemented by the wood top on the hutch and the gold granite of the counters.

Elaborate moldings, massive fluted columns and beaded inset-styled doors add detail and dimension to the cabinetry. The chestnut-toned cherry island adds visual contrast and abundant storage space while conveniently concealing a microwave and dishwasher. The cherry hutch balances the island and provides a place for displaying the homeowners' treasured collection of stemware and other tableware.

The interior of the hood area is covered in a yellow glazed tile accented by hand-painted decorative flower tiles. A soothing ambiance is created by a pair of matching rustic chandeliers, one over the island, the other over the dining table. Under-cabinet lighting, recessed hi-hats and low-voltage in-cabinet fixtures complete the illumination. Hardware in crackled porcelain and antique pewter provides a finishing touch.

The combination of natural elements and well-appointed features provides this couple with a relaxing atmosphere to enjoy with friends and family. ◆

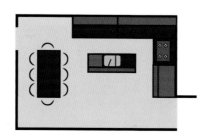

Special Features:
Custom hood with fluted pillars, large furniture styled island, custom cherry hutch and antique glazed cabinetry, granite countertops with hand painted tile backsplash.

Dimensions:
14' X 19'

Products Used:
Cabinetry: Custom
Flooring: Oak Hardwood
Countertops: Akropolis Marble & Granite New Venetian Gold
Sink(s): Franke
Faucets: Whitehaus
Dishwasher: KitchenAid
Stove: Thermador
Lighting: Seagull
Refrigerator: KitchenAid
Knobs: Top Knobs
Tile: Antigua

DESIGNER

Christian Manzo
Renaissance Kitchen & Bath
663 Skippack Pike
Blue Bell, PA 19422
215-542-5000

A modern rendition of a classic shaker cabinet.

variation on a
classic

Special Features:
The designer's trademark look ties a group of cabinet doors into a singular design.

Dimensions:
16' X 28'

Products Used:
Cabinetry: Custom Cabinets
Countertops: Juparana Topazi Granite
Sink(s): Kindred
Faucets: Grohe
Dishwasher: Bosch
Cooktop: Existing
Hood: Thermador
Refrigerator: Sub-Zero
Oven: Thermador
Cabinet Hardware: Hafele
Windows and Doors: Marvin

When the owners of this Bay Area home decided to remodel their cramped, outdated kitchen, they knew where to turn. They were already well acquainted with Marilyn C Gardunio, of J.B. Turner & Sons. Gardunio has redesigned their master suite the previous year. With confidence in Gardunio's talent as a designer, they allowed her the freedom to fully develop her ideas for their new space.

The remodel of this 1940s home included a new home office, laundry room, and guest bath. The centerpiece of the project was the kitchen. The homeowners, parents of boys 2 and 10, wanted the kitchen to be a casual space for friends and family to gather. To meet this request, the designer created a ;large central island around which quest can congregate and socialize as the homeowner cooks. There is also a small TV area with a loveseat where the two boys can stay nearby while the family meal is being prepared.

The designer then turned eye towards the artistic elements of the kitchen. The designer created her trademark look, which is a simple shaker door with a modern twist. The cabinets are grouped together with a singular design. To create this unique design Gardunio turned to business partner and contractor John(who is also her husband) and their son Sean to build her ideas for this new design.

The homeowners now have a beautiful, inviting kitchen to share with family and friends. ◆

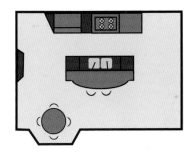

Photographer: Oleg March

A butler's pantry was created in a historic mansion.

old-world
grandeur

Designed by Walker & Gillette in 1918, the mansion was constructed in Regency style with Gothic elements. Leaded stained glass, hand-carved oak furniture and other period elements worthy of the structure took their places in this home that now functions as a museum in Oyster Bay, New York, The mansion was chosen as the Decorator Showhouse in 1997 at Coe Hall Planting Fields Arboretum State Historic Park. Since the museum opened in 1978 the second-floor rooms had been closed to the public. Now they would welcome visitors, and recreating the elegant atmosphere of the affluent period was a challenge.

Certified Kitchen Designer Rochelle Kalisch took on the task of transforming two small spaces—a bathroom and a powder room—into a functional butler's pantry adjoining a dining room. It is only coincidence that Kalisch's company is called Regency Kitchens, but now her challenge was exactly that.

The bathroom had a beautiful leaded window that was partially blocked by a wall. Removing that wall allowed light to flood through the window; removing the partition between the two rooms created a workable space. Two existing doors accommodate the flow of museum visitors.

Custom 10-foot cabinets with Gothic doors and leaded glass inserts are perfectly in keeping with the architecture and grandeur of the great mansion. A fresh touch comes from a blueberry glaze on the maple wood. The carpet-like terra cotta in the center of the floor, surrounded by the jewel tones of the other tiles maintains the old-world sparkle and warmth. All the accessories and other elements reflect the original era of this magnificent home, while creating an inviting and functional space. ◆

Special Features:
The kitchen was designed for a historic landmark mansion. The custom- blueberry glazed cabinetry with gothic door style and leaded glass inserts, are all in keeping with the architecture of this great building.

Dimensions:
13' X 9'

Products Used:
Cabinetry: Regency Kitchen's
Flooring & Backsplash: Ann Sacks Tile
Countertops: International Stone & Accesories
Sinks: Herbeau
Faucets: Herbeau
Lighting: V/C Lighting-Juno
Refrigerator: Sub-Zero 200 Series
Oven: MW- GE

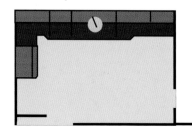

DESIGNER

Rochelle Kalisch
Regency Kitchens
4204 14th Ave.
Brooklyn, NY 11219
718-435-4266
And
204 E. 77th St., Ste.1E
New York, NY 10021
212-517-8707

DESIGNER

Michael Teipen
CKD, CBD and
Kristen Zwitt are
design professionals
with Kitchens by
Teipen. Contact the
designers at
Kitchens by Teipen, Inc.
1035 N. State Road 135
Greenwood, IN 46412
317-888-7345

> The designers
> were able to
> combine the
> future with
> the past.

Photographer: Michael Teipen

Special Features:
Custom built one piece
canopy that mimics the
island design. Special
window seat with
matching cherry wood
top and doors access
the bottom cabinets.

Dimensions:
22' x 16'

Products Used:
Cabinetry: Kitchen
Jewels
Flooring: Excazare Talc
Florida Tile
Countertops: Labrador
Antique Granite on
island and perimeter,
Black Galaxy Granite
on bar and desk.
Sink(s): Eljer
Faucets: Kohler Antique
Dishwasher: Asko
Cooktop: Thermador
Gas 5 Burner
Lighting: WAC Under
cabinet lighting and
canopy, recessed cans
in the ceiling
Refrigerator: Sub-Zero
650 and Sub-Zero
700BR
Wall Covering: Faux
Finishing
Oven: Thermador
Double Ovens

history, function
and technology

This home, built in 1906, is listed in the National Historic Register. Originally it served as quarters for higher-ranking officers at Fort Benjamin Harrison in Indianapolis. A certain responsibility rests with owners of historic properties, and these homeowners wanted to combine the look of the early twentieth century with the function and technology of a kitchen designed for the new millennium. Generous work surfaces for catered events, hiding some permanent obstructions, multiple display areas and multiple workstations were some of the requests the clients brought to kitchen designers Michael Teipen and Kristen Zwitt, of Kitchens by Teipen, Inc. The two welcomed this unique opportunity to combine the future with the past.

The kitchen was relatively small, with large windows, many entries and a huge chimney to hide. A separate butler's pantry and enclosed walkway consumed potentially useful space, which was reclaimed by eliminating the pantry and the walkway walls.

An angled wall was added to camouflage the chimney and provide a more functional work surface. The multi-level island features table-height seating for two, along with a large cooktop, vegetable sink, raised open shelves for display and matching canopy with display niches floating on fluted columns. A furniture hutch and a work desk were designed to frame the rear entry. A large wainscot chase next to the desk area encloses the plumbing pipes supplying the second floor. Display space for the homeowners' collections of pie vents, porcelain and other art was discovered above the dining room hutch. The wet bar has been positioned near the front hall for ease of access and to minimize disruption in the food-preparation areas.

Granite countertops, antique-look faucets and skillful use of illumination make the room a tribute to both centuries. ◆

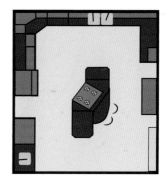

He wanted an airy, open kitchen with an old-world feel.

a dramatic
solution

The client, a single father of two children, wanted an airy, open kitchen with views of the outdoors, a place for easy conversation with kids and guests, yet warm and traditional with an old-world feel. Clutter should be hidden, especially during business parties. He presented this challenge to Haskell Matheny of Haskell Interiors, LLC, for his recently purchased condominium in a golf-course community.

Haskell removed the wall between the galley kitchen and great room. In its place he designed an island 14 feet wide and 16 feet high to serve as a dramatic display storage unit and serving bar on one side, a functional work island on the other. With the inspiration of Classical architecture, the designer created the island in cherry wood with gold-leaf accents and a dramatic multispecies veneer sunburst for the great room. This tied in with the bookcases and fireplace mantel, which he had also designed. For the island's kitchen side, he used maple with custom carvings, granite and limestone.

The focal point is the custom mantel hood, made in wood and finished to match the limestone backsplash. Hidden storage is abundant. The hood's carved legs pull out for spice and condiment storage. The block "quoins" on the base corners of the island pull out to store food on the kitchen side, videotapes on the great room side. A TV is hidden next to the hood, while appliance garages are hidden on the kitchen side of the illuminated glass doors.

The kitchen has professional appliances, two full-size sinks, antique-style faucets and custom tile backsplash, which features tufted limestone with Italian carved wooden buttons, accented with green mosaic marble and a hand-carved and hand-painted center medallion tile with hammered copper squares. Antique copper cabinet hardware with crackle porcelain completes the look.

The final design functions well and satisfies all the homeowner's needs. And the dramatic solution is always a great conversation-starter at his parties. ◆

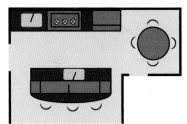

Special Features:
Custom designed hood with pull-outs for spices. Limestone backsplash with tufted designs; antiqued gold leaf accents; architectural styling of island; inlaid veneer sunburst on island pediment.

Dimensions:
22' X 11'

Products Used:
Cabinetry: custom designed by Haskell Interiors
Flooring: wood, oak with honey stain
Countertops: granite- "Gallo Cabaca", Verda Oriental- bar top
Sink(s): Whitehaus 36" farmhouse
Faucets: Herbeau in weathered copper; Whitehaus in oil bronze
Dishwasher: Asko with custom wood panel
Cooktop: 48" Viking Professional
Lighting: Juno recess and cabinetry lights
Refrigerator: Amana 48" built in with custom panels and carved top
Wall Covering: Benjamin Moore Paint
Hood: custom design with limestone finish and spice pullouts

DESIGNER

Haskell Matheny
Haskell Interiors
85 First Street N.W.
Cleveland, TN 37311
423-472-6409

A brick fire-place and hearth add to the eclectic mix.

a new england
farmhouse

On a quiet back road just outside the resort town of Stowe, Vermont, lies a lovely farmhouse with beautiful grounds and tremendous curb appeal. For all its charms, this home was in dire need of interior renovations and updating—including the kitchen area.

The homeowners enjoy gourmet cooking and frequent entertaining. They wanted a kitchen where they could combine these activities in a space that was classy and elegant, yet comfortable. The rooms that now comprise the kitchen were a small sitting area and kitchen and an oversized utility room. These were separated by a stairway, making a crowded and inconvenient space. Low ceilings and rounded beams created additional design challenges.

The homeowners sought the professional expertise of designer Matt Grundy of Builder Specialties, Inc., to help them transform this problem space into a dream kitchen. The design solution involved removing the stairway to make one large open space.

Custom cherry cabinets with an earthtone stain/glaze combination were installed. The mild distressing and sand-over corners create a feel of casual elegance. A 12 by 4-foot island with 3-inch maple butcherblock top was created for food preparation and dining. The main sink is located at the end of the island.

Working closely with the homeowners, the designer added a long run of cabinetry that houses a pantry, refrigerator and wet bar. Staggered depths, reeded columns and curved-front cabinets add interest while visually breaking up the long lines.

Dark green granite countertops were specified to contrast with the light maple island top; stacked crown molding was hard-carved around the exposed beams. Tile flooring and backsplash, a brick fireplace and hearth and an arched stone canopy over the commercial range add to the eclectic mix, while the owners' keen decorating sense provides the final touches to this beautiful room. ◆

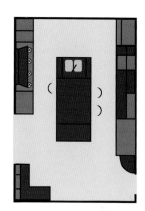

Special Features:
Farmhouse Butcherblock Table Island, Arched Stone Canopy over Range, Staggered Depths, Reeded Columns and Curved Front Cabinets add Interest and Breakup Long Runs.

Dimensions:
15' X 31'

Products Used:
Cabinetry: Omega Custom
Countertops: Verde Candais Granite And Maple Butcherblock
Sink(s): American Standard Main Sink, Kindred Bar Sink
Range Oven: Garland Range, Frigidaire Oven and Warming Drawer
Refrigerator: Amana Stainless Steel

DESIGNER

Matt Grundy
Builder Specialties Inc.
92 River St.
Montpelier, VT 05602
802-223-5583

DESIGNER

Randall Shaw
Nordic Kitchens &
Bath Inc.
4437 Veterans Blvd.
Metairie, LA 70006
504-888-2300

photography: Richard Vallon

> A serious cook
> needs a serious
> kitchen.

new orleans
style

Special Features:
Elevated counter
height, 38", Custom
copper hood, Custom
8x8 wine rack

Dimensions:
17' X 23'

Products Used:
Cabinetry: Wood
Harbor
Flooring: Stained con-
crete
Countertops: Granite
3cm Giallo Veneziano
Sink(s): Elkay
Faucets: Grohe
Dishwasher: Gaggenau
Cooktop: Gaggenau
Lighting: Recessed cans
Refrigerator: Sub-Zero
Oven: Gaggenau /
Thermador
Icemaker: KitchenAid
Wall tile: Latco

When it came time for these homeowners to build their own kitchen, they didn't exactly start from square one. They're owners of a restaurant in New Orleans' French Quarter—an area known for excellent cuisine. And even when they're away from the restaurant, they love to cook. So when they came to Randall L. Shaw of Nordic Kitchens & Baths, Inc., they had a well-developed wish list. High on that list were appliances.

The couple has children who are grown and do not live at home, but they do entertain frequently. They needed a welcoming space for guests to mingle.

Having plenty of kitchen experience, they knew exactly how high their counters should be; they specified 38 inches for maximum ease and comfort.

They wanted a large table/island at counter height where they could prepare food, converse and, at times, enjoy dining. That countertop is rustic pine and all others are 3cm granite.

Stylish stained concrete was chosen for the flooring.

Now it was time for those all-important appliances. These include two separate ovens, a four-burner gas cooktop, a grill, a deep fryer,

a warming drawer, a microwave, a 48-inch refrigerator, an icemaker and—of course—a dishwasher. These were all positioned with a view for ergonomics and easy traffic flow. In addition, the couple wanted to incorporate a large, three-compartment sink that they already owned.

All major elements in place, the homeowners and the designer turned to matters of style and accents. A custom copper hood contributes to the warmth and welcome of the space. A unique bar with a custom wine rack was a charming addition and a convenience when entertaining. Spice storage was placed on the wall behind the cooktop and to the left of the cooktop.

Now they're ready to welcome guests in true New Orleans style. ◆

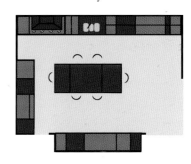

DESIGNER

Gary Lazzaro
Kitchen & Bath
Expressions
1175 Ridge Road
Webster, NY 14580
716-872-6130

Photographer: Mike Gaglio

Angled cabinets facilitate easy travel.

a user-friendly
kitchen

Special Features:
Elliptical dome cabinet with tinted beveled glass, "Fly-over" over Kitchen sink, Multi-level cabinetry, Faucet located over range for filling large pots, Accented top trim molding, Decorative columns in island

Dimensions:
21' X 16'

Products Used:
Cabinetry: Dura Supreme- Cherry
Flooring: Granite Tile
Countertops: Granite: Gialo Veneziano
Sink(s): Blanco stainless steel undermount
Dishwasher: Bosch
Range: Viking: 48: Stainless
Refrigerator: KitchenAid, Stainless steel 42" Built-in
Cabinet Hardware: Top Knobs
Range Hood: Viking

Through careful planning, designer and remodeler Gary Lazzaro of Kitchen & Bath Expressions was able to accommodate everything on his client's wish list for the kitchen in her new home. A user-friendly preparation and cooking area was a must for this avid cook. The angled cabinets facilitate easy travel, as well as an aesthetically pleasing atmosphere for entertaining.

The designer utilized Dura Supreme cabinetry, blending several amenities into a gourmet food preparation area. Cherry cabinets with warm Harvest stain, Wild Cherry-stained top trim for accent and raised panel doors create an elegant look. Continuity between the granite countertops and the cherry cabinetry was achieved with granite knobs on the cabinets.

A center island was created to serve as a food-preparation area, complete with a pull-out cutting board built into the base cabinet and roll-out shelves for easy access to cookware. The granite island countertop also makes a good serving area when the homeowner entertains.

One special feature is a convenient water faucet to fill large pots for cooking, locat-ed between the 48-inch stainless-steel range and range hood.

Incorporated into the base cabinets are more roll-out shelves, tray dividers next to the range, tilt-down trays and a pull-out waste bin beneath the sink. Recycle bins are situated in the base cabinet to the right of the sink.

The Blanco double-bowl undermount stainless-steel sink complements the stainless-steel fronts of the 42-inch KitchenAid refrigerator and the Bosch dishwasher—appliances selected in part because of the Energy Star® label for meeting energy-efficient, cost-saving guidelines.

A desk area has been created with organizer shelves concealed behind doors. The round-top cabinet above the desk is perfect for the display of special decorative pieces.◆

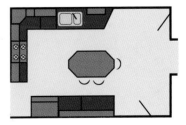

DESIGNER

Carol Lindell is a principal designer and owner of DCI Kitchen and Bath. Contact the designer at DCI Kitchen and Bath, 1323 Matthews Mint Hill Rd., Matthews, NC 28105, 704/846-1322.

Several seating areas, open bookcases, and wine cubbies beckon family and friends into this Country French kitchen.

nature indoors

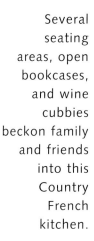

Special Features
Custom cooking center with wood hood.
Large multi-level island.
Raised dishwasher furniture hutch.

Dimensions
18 feet by 25 feet

Products Used
Cabinetry: Quality Custom Cabinetry;
Flooring: Oak;
Countertops: Corian - Canyon Summit;
Dishwasher: KitchenAid; Cooktop: KitchenAid;
Refrigerator: KitchenAid;
Oven: KitchenAid

Country French warmth and elegance is evident throughout the open design of this custom built home, conceived and constructed by a builder for his family amid the rolling acreage, streams and forests of North Carolina. From the home's front entry, guests move directly into the family-sized kitchen where expansive windows overlook a large wrap-around porch and nearby stream.

The challenge presented to Carol Lindell of Design Centers International/DCI Kitchen and Bath, was to create a kitchen made of materials, colors and finishes that would echo the great outdoors. To accomplish this, Lindell selected a curved maple hood to dominate the heart of the cooking center, majestically hovering over the cooktop and built-in oven. Open wall cabinets with graceful, carved valances and bead board interiors flank the maple hood, extending to the built-in Kitchen Aid refrigerator and large pantry/larder on either side.

A large island was selected to accommodate food preparation and cleanup, as well as to provide ample storage and seating area. Included in the island are a raised dishwasher and undercounter microwave, storage for dishes, wine cubbies and an open bookcase.

The nearby Country French hutch echoes the colors and styling of the Butternut glazed maple cabinetry along the cooking center and the Olde Towne Moss island. Chicken wire inserts, carved edges, bead board, and turned feet invoke the look and feel of fine custom furniture.

This magnificent design results in a warm and natural looking kitchen that beckons family and friends as soon as they walk through the front door. ◆

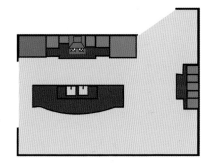

DESIGNER

John Lang is a design-
er with Lang's
Signature Kitchen and
Bath. Contact the
designer at Lang's
Signature Kitchen and
Bath, 2021
Nottingham Way,
Mercerville, NJ,
609/587-7880.

> All of the major appliances now have a home in this open and fashionable space.

metallic warmth

Special Features
Stone enclosed cooking area with copper countertops. Copper deco tiles in floor and on backsplash.

Dimensions
23 feet by 13 feet

Products Used
Cabinetry: Jay Rambo Custom Cabinetry; Backsplash and Flooring: Ceramic Tile by Charles Tile; Countertops: Granite; Sink: Whitehaus; Faucets Grohe; Dishwasher: KitchenAid Range: Viking; Lighting: Task Brand Low Voltage Lights.

For this homeowner who entertains often, having a kitchen with plenty of open space was of optimum importance. Additionally, the homeowners longed for a functional kitchen with abundant work surfaces and top-of-the-line appliances.

John Lang, professional designer with Lang's Signature Kitchen & Bath, knew that the only way to create a kitchen to meet his client's needs was to fully gut the entire space enabling a complete remodel and redesign.

First, the wall in the center of the kitchen was removed creating a more open floor plan. Due to the room's long and narrow dimensions it was difficult to

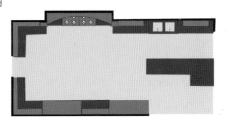

place all of the major appliances the client desired within this limited layout. To solve the problem, Lang bumped out a 78" space from the kitchen to accommodate the 48" Viking range. A long island sporting granite countertops was placed close to the sink to provide easy accessibility and abundant work space, while additionally creating an eating area for the homeowner's daily use.

One of the most magnificent features of this kitchen transformation is its stone enclosed cooking area with copper countertops. The cool look of copper makes its appearance in other carefully selected spots including the ceramic deco floor tiles and backsplash above the stainless steel range. The shimmer of stainless steel is highlighted on the chairs surrounding the island's eating area as well.

In the end, the designer was able to create an open and airy kitchen space with just the right accents of metal....for a uniquely customized look! ◆

Photographer: Steve Whitsitt

An eased archway and special lighting add dramatic appeal.

joyous
juxtaposition

Special Features:
Marble countertop on the island was original to the building; stone was reworked for the island. The open area above the sink was set aside to display original art work.

Dimensions:
15' x 15'

Products Used:
Cabinetry: Neff
Flooring: Black stainedBrazilian cherry
Countertops: Absolute black granite
Sink(s): Franke
Faucets: Grohe
Dishwasher: Bosch
Range: Thermadore
Lighting: Neff
Refrigerator: Sub-Zero

An upscale urban loft in the heart of Rock Hill, S.C., may seem like a paradox, but it's not. A notable artist provided for the reclamation of a landmark building in the city to be converted into condominiums, with the top floor as her own residence. She contracted with Jeanine DeVaney of Charlotte In-Vironments to provide space planning and kitchen design, and Design Centers International, DCI Kitchen & Bath for cabinetry, countertops and custom installation. The success of the kitchen was achieved through contrasts, textures and lighting.

The client wanted an open floor plan, and the kitchen evolved into a major design focus. The immense arched windows and 14-foot ceilings of the old building provided a surprising juxtaposition with the high-tech kitchen. Pro-line stainless steel appliances, high-gloss Neff laminate burlwood cabinets, black granite countertops and a black ceiling meet with dramatic lighting to create a space with theatrical grandeur.

The kitchen's focal point is an eased arch that repeats the arch of the old windows. The range and contemporary styled hood sets the stage for a gourmet cooking center. Halogen arc lamps gracefully illuminate and accentuate the beauty of the cabinetry.

With teamwork, overall success was ensured. The project results not only respected more than 100 years of history within the old bank building, but also met the client's desires for a special loft home.◆

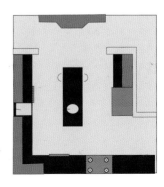

DESIGNER

John V. Testa
Kitchen Concepts
210 Daniel Webster Hwy.
Nashua, NH 03060
603.891.2600

Photographer: John V. Testa

Skylights and oak floors create natural warmth.

new
millennium

Special Features:
Large multi-function island; natural cherry cabinets; bump-out for new window and skylights

Dimensions:
16' x 21'

Products Used:
Cabinetry: Wildwood
Flooring: Natural oak
Countertops: Laurentide granite
Sink(s): Kindrid
Faucets: KWC
Dishwasher: KitchenAid Professional Series
Cooktop: KitchenAid
Lighting: Pendants and recess
Refrigerator: KitchenAid Professional Series
Wallcovering: Paint
Oven: KitchenAid
Wine Cooler: KitchenAid
Warming Drawer: KitchenAid
Skylights: Anderson

The owners of this 25-year-old Hollis, N.H., home are Florida natives with grown children. The Southern-style home badly needed an update to reflect the couple's changing lifestyle.

Bumping the back wall 6 feet, moving the door from the garage, installing four skylights and a new angled wall with an Anderson window brought the antiquated kitchen into the new millennium. New oak floors that flow throughout the entire first floor, natural cherry cabinets and Laurentide granite countertops make this a comfortable place not just for cooking, but also for relaxing with friends.

The large multi-use center island is the key element of the kitchen. This spacious area provides a place for the busy couple to enjoy their morning coffee and a quick look at the newspaper, have a casual meal, and work on bills and other paperwork. It includes work areas on either side of the gas cooktop and a wine cooler that stores up to 60 bottles.

Multiple work stations throughout the kitchen allow a couple of cooks to work side by side at the same time, so food preparation can be a mutually rewarding activity. A warming drawer was added to preserve home-cooked meals for latecomers and to make entertaining a breeze.

When all was said and done, Kitchen Concepts of Nashua, N.H., had transformed the dark, 1970s kitchen into a functional, contemporary room.◆

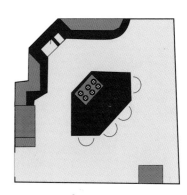

Photographer: Matthew Lausé

Cabinets vary in height and include lots of detail.

tall order

This new kitchen was specifically designed to meet the aesthetic and functional needs of the clients, owners of a commercial construction company in Ohio. They wanted a beautiful space for entertaining and a functional area for food prep and cooking. The family is a large one, not in numbers, but the couple and their two teenage boys all are very tall, which was a consideration in the kitchen's construction.

Designer Pamela McKiernan of Living Spaces Custom Design expanded the sink area by elevating the main sink pass-thru to 40 inches high. This area includes a large double sink, dishwasher, trash pull-out and drawer-base cabinets. Both ends of the cabinets were left open for display.

One side of the 36-inch-high island includes a 31-inch-high recess for baking. The other side of the island has a large single sink, second trash pull-out and warming drawer. Open radius display cabinets at both ends complete the island.

The homeowners expressed a strong desire for crown detail, so the designer used a combination 12-inch crown build-up. Cabinet heights varied from 96 inches to 120 inches. Throughout the kitchen, designers used a bulky 5-by-5-inch furniture leg, custom arched raised panels over the double oven, hood and two open hutch cabinets. The color palette was a natural cherry, and the complementing island was a maple custom paint, antiqued and distressed. Doors and drawers were beaded inset.

The result was a gorgeous design that catered to the clients' interests and served the needs of the family. ◆

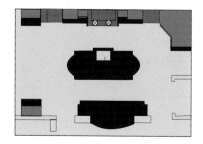

Special Features:
Separate refrigerator and freezer; two-tiered island; pass-thru with double sink and dishwasher

Dimensions:
16' x 37' 8"

Products Used:
Cabinetry: Plain-N-Fancy Custom Cabinets
Flooring: Tile
Countertops: Dakota Mahogany granite
Sink(s): Elkay steel under-mount
Faucets: Moen
Dishwasher: Asko
Cooktop: Thermador
Lighting: Cans and pendant
Refrigerator: Sub-Zero 700 Series
Wallcovering: Paint
Oven: Thermador
Warming Drawer: Thermador
Hood: Thermador

DESIGNER

Pamela S. McKiernan
Living Spaces Custom
Design Inc.
350 E. Main St.
Batavia, OH 45103
513.735.2393

DESIGNER

Patrick H. Ryan, CKD
Kitchen Concepts Inc.
10868 Kenwood Road
Cincinnati, OH 45242
513.531.3838

Photographer: Steve Whitsitt

Cherry cabinets coordinate well with green countertops.

entertaining
delight

Special Features:
Task ceiling and under-cabinet lighting; built-in wet bar; functional island

Dimensions:
13' x 29'

Products Used:
Cabinetry: Kitchen Craft Cherry Bridgewater
Flooring: Select Oak hardwood
Countertops: Corian Malachite
Sink(s): Corian Bisque
Faucets: KWC, Opella
Dishwasher: KitchenAid
Cooktop: Dacor
Lighting: Task ceiling lights, Alkco undercabinet lighting
Refrigerator: Sub-Zero
Oven: Dacor double ovens
Compactor: KitchenAid
Wine Cooler: Marvel
Wall Tile: Jasba "cottage" with Kitchen Motif inserts

Homeowners of this Cincinnati residence were desperate to change their drab, dingy 1970s kitchen into a bright, functional room. The original cabinets were extremely dark, and the flooring was worn vinyl. The clients wanted to create an appealing environment for entertaining with a better flow throughout the family and outdoor rooms. Knowing the kitchen was in need of a facelift, designer Patrick H. Ryan of Kitchen Concepts Inc. came to the rescue.

More than 15 ceiling and under-cabinet lights give life to the once gloomy area. Since the original island was too bulky, Ryan worked to trim it to a more manageable size and, thus, make it easier to maneuver around. To save space in other places, narrower appliances, such as a counter-depth refrigerator, were installed to create nearly 6 inches of extra space, every inch providing more room for cooking, cleaning and interacting in the kitchen. Ideal for entertaining, a built-in wet bar provides additional room for

storing wine and other party goods. The location of the bar continues the idea of flow and openness from the kitchen to the family room. Solid cherry wood cabinetry and green Corian countertops signify elegance, functionality and quality that will last through many celebrations at the home. Ryan says he saw this project not as a challenge, but as part of his ability to bring satisfaction to his customers.◆

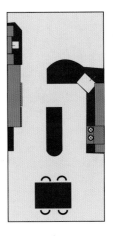

Plenty of storage and counter space transforms this kitchen into a cooking paradise.

structural
divide

The challenge to this home's redesign was to create a truly functional kitchen with an adjacent dining room for casual entertaining as well as formal dining. In order to accomplish this, certified kitchen designer Jeff Boico combined four small rooms by moving load-bearing walls, relocating windows, adding a door to the backyard, and moving the powder room down the hall.

The resulting U-shaped kitchen, with its angled peninsula counter, earth-tone color palette, and maple cabinets create a warm and inviting feel. Complete with storage and counter space, the glass and stainless steel roll-out shelves and bins in the base cabinets not only help to keep the kitchen organized, but also put everything within reach.

A 'magic' corner base cabinet, featuring a unique pull-out storage, makes the most of an otherwise unused corner space. A tall larder pantry standing adjacent to the refrigerator provides plenty of storage space for boxed, canned and other food items.

Top-of-the-line appliances, including a 42" Sub Zero refrigerator, Thermador cooktop and Bosch double ovens combine to create a cooking paradise for the homeowners, while the peninsula's casual dining area serves double duty as a buffet.

The gentle flowing of details in the cabinetry's crown molding tops, custom tile backsplash, and pendant lights, which casts just the right illumination on the peninsula, top off this divine kitchen space for the perfect dining environment...whatever your mood! ◆

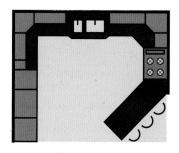

Special Features
Angled peninsula. Integrated microwave cabinet. Accent lighting over peninsula. Accented angles around sink base. Tile backsplash with custom designer border.

Dimensions
12 feet by 15 feet

Products Used
Cabinetry: Neff; Flooring: Ceramic Tile; Countertops: Granite – Pink Fiorito; Sink: Franke with stainless steel undermount; Faucet: Franke; Dishwasher: Miele; Cooktop: Thermador; Lighting: Recessed high hats; Refrigerator: Sub Zero overlay, 42"; Wallcovering: Custom pained by Ray Rolling; Double Oven: Bosch.

DESIGNER

Jeff Boico is a design professional and Vice-President of Classic Kitchen and Bath Center, Ltd. Contact the designer at Classic Kitchen & Bath Center, Ltd., 1062 Northern Blvd., Roslyn, NY 11576; 516/621-7700.

DESIGNER

Don Boico is a design professional and Owner of Classic Kitchen & Bath Center, Ltd., 1062 Northern Blvd., Roslyn, NY 11576; 516/621-7700.

Special attention is paid to the careful blending of the appliances into the design.

smooth and slick

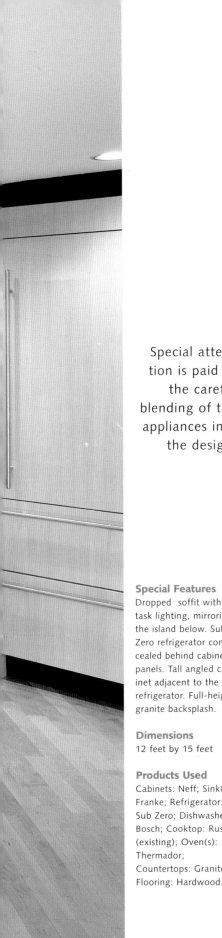

Special Features
Dropped soffit with task lighting, mirroring the island below. Sub Zero refrigerator concealed behind cabinet panels. Tall angled cabinet adjacent to the refrigerator. Full-height granite backsplash.

Dimensions
12 feet by 15 feet

Products Used
Cabinets: Neff; Sink(s): Franke; Refrigerator: Sub Zero; Dishwasher: Bosch; Cooktop: Russell (existing); Oven(s): Thermador; Countertops: Granite; Flooring: Hardwood.

Desiring a kitchen that would be aesthetically pleasing as well as functional, these homeowners enlisted the professional design services of Don Boico, CKD, CR, President of Classic Kitchen & Bath Center, Ltd., to turn their 12' x 15' space into a sleek, contemporary masterpiece.

Boico remodeled the space by closing off an entryway to the kitchen creating an L-shape design, which also prevented household traffic from passing through the cook's work space. Ensuring that the

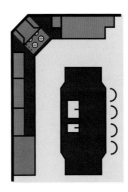

kitchen appliances blended well into the design, Boico integrated the Sub Zero refrigerator with matching cabinet doors and drawers. The black wall ovens and microwave complement the dark counter surfaces and black trim on the cabinet end panels.

Designed to serve many purposes, the kitchen's island creates an ideal food preparation area, ample space for casual dining, and a convenient area for a buffet...not to mention offering great views of the waterway that passes behind the house. The island's shape is mirrored in the unique dropped soffit above.

An abundance of wall and base cabinet storage ensures a place for every item in this contemporary kitchen, while a tall, glass-fronted cabinet adjacent to the refrigerator allows the homeowners to conveniently display their elegant crystal and glassware. All this makes for a magnificently functional yet beautiful kitchen redesign, suitable for the most contemporary of tastes. ◆

Every appliance is surrounded by the elegance of custom glazed cabinets, hand carved corbels, and granite countertops.

winning
european design

Designed to be the feature attraction in a European Country style Parade of Homes entry for an award-winning custom home builder, the homeowner and his interior designer wanted a kitchen that would set their entry apart from all of the other homes competing in the $1 million+ category.

The builder envisioned the area around the professional style range as the focal point to the kitchen, providing the setting for an old European hearth. He also wanted the cabinetry to look as if it had been in place for centuries.

Amy Norris, CKD, professional designer with Triangle Design Kitchens, accomplished this by incorporating a wainscoted hood surround with mantle, hand-carved corbels, and columnar cabinets leading down to the granite countertops. The side cabinets, containing slide-out racks to hold spices and other condiments, make these items easily accessible. The cabinetry is finished in a custom glaze over white paint for a worn, warm and inviting look.

Multiple moldings stacked at the top of the cabinets add the finishing touch to this elegant room.

Further complementing its unique charm are a multi-level island with seating for four, a raised dishwasher for easier access, and every conceivable appliance a serious gourmet cook and entertainer could ever desire, including a warming drawer and wine cellar.

All of the designer's painstaking details paid off...with this beautiful kitchen winning the Special Feature Award, along with a Gold Award for the entire home. ◆

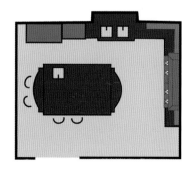

Special Features
Raised dishwasher.
Multi-level counter on island.
Hand made ceramic tile backsplashes.

Dimensions
16 feet by 16 feet

Products Used
Cabinetry: Plain and Fancy Custom Cabinetry; Flooring: Hardwood; Countertops: Granite; Dishwasher: Asko; Range: Viking; Lighting: Hera Lighting; Refrigerator: SubZero; Wallcovering: Paint; Other: Warming Drawer - Viking, Wine Cellar - Marvel.

DESIGNER

Amy Norris, CKD, is a
designer with Triangle
Design Kitchens, Inc.
Contact the designer
at Triangle Design
Kitchens, Inc., 5216
Holly Ridge Dr.,
Raleigh, NC 27612,
919/787-0256.

Photographer: Melabee Miller

The high-spout
faucet brings
back memories.

needs and nostalgia

Designer Steven Joel Meltzer of Abbey's Kitchens Baths & Interiors, Inc., enjoys telling the story of this stylish kitchen.

In his 25 years of designing kitchens, a handful of special clients have made it truly rewarding to be involved in the roller-coaster world of kitchen and bath design. The designs pictured here are part of a joint effort between client and designer. Only sometimes do you find the enthusiasm and zeal that were evident on this project.

From the first interview to the final coat of paint, there was a sense of purpose and understanding among all those involved. It is important that clients realize that unforeseen situations arise during a project. There must be a mutual respect among the designer, clients and tradespeople. When that respect exists, all involved will work together to find a peaceful solution to any such situations. Right from the start, the clients (he an executive with a major communications company, she a retired computer consultant and now a full-time mom) knew exactly what they wanted. Colors, function, appliance needs (she loves to bake and prepare gourmet meals) were all care-fully researched, calling upon the knowledge of the designer and Internet technology.

Not all the aspects of the design were dictated by wants and needs. In this room's planning, a bit of nostalgia came into play. Years before the clients became a family of five, the husband and wife met in college, where they both worked in a campus bar and restaurant. The memory of using that high-spout commercial faucet back in the kitchen brought back the good times of their college years. Hence, look for a high-spout faucet on the main sink in the kitchen island. Client enthusiasm, participation, understanding, cooperation—and a bit of nostalgia added into the recipe. What more could any designer ask for? ◆

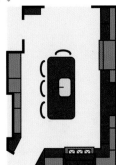

Special Features:
Full extension drawers for easy access to all base cabinets, shallow tall storage

Dimensions:
19 feet x 14 feet

Products Used:
Cabinetry: Abbey's custom designed; Flooring: Forbo Marmoleum linoleum squares; Countertops: Bedrock granite "White Wave"; Sink(s): Whitehaus Custom Chef; Faucets: Kohler Culinary main sink, Opella prep sink; Dishwashers: Miele; Cooktop/oven: DCS; Lighting: Task Zenon, DMF downlighting; Refrigerator: Kitchen Aid stainless steel; Wallcovering: custom painting by Lalaynia; Custom hood: Vent-A-Hood; Backsplash: Peach Travertine, Standard Tile Corp.

DESIGNER

Steven Joel Meltzer,
Abbey's Kitchens
Baths & Interiors, Inc.,
38 Chatham Road,
Suite 4, Short Hills, NJ
07078; 973/376-8878

DESIGNER

Mary Maier Galloway,
CKD, IIDA, NKBA,
Kitchen Classics by
Custom Crafters, Inc.,
6023 Wilson Blvd.,
Arlington, VA 22205;
703/532-7000.

Photographer: Jack Neith

Warmth and elegance in a light-filled kitchen.

Special Features:
Arched valances and double crown molding link windows, corner cabinets with interior lighting, "command center" computer station with keyboard tray and telephone/fax

Dimensions:
15 feet x 21 feet

Products Used:
Cabinetry: Dura Supreme, Alectra Series in Satin White; Flooring: Red oak wood strip; Counters: 3cm Verde Butterfly granite; Sink: Elkay; Faucets: Kohler Fairfax Polished Brass Vibrant; Dishwasher: GE Quiet Power II; Cooktop: Jenn-Air 30" with downdraft; Lighting: CSL under-cabinet, Progress recessed; Refrigerator: KitchenAid side-by-side with dispenser; Oven: KitchenAid thermal and convection; Microwave: GE; Other: Hinckley pendant light

entertaining pleasure

Entertaining in a warm, elegant kitchen was what this couple wanted. They'd just moved to Virginia for a high-level position in telecommunications. There would be parties and gatherings. They also asked for morning light.

Designer Mary Maier Galloway completely reconfigured the kitchen to allow a 6-foot window to be installed on the east side, matching the one on the north wall above the sink. This permitted both early light and a view of the beautiful back yard.

The two large spans of glass now presented a challenge: how to integrate them into the kitchen cabinet design. Galloway's solution was to create matching arched valances with keystones to hide the central joints that were necessary for spans of such length. The fabric chosen for the valances pulls in colors from nearby decorative finishes.

The double oven and refrigerator were moved to the inside wall with easy access to the central island. Two corner cabinets, with glass doors and shelves, anchor the arched spans on either side of the sink. Their interior low-voltage halogen lights add sparkle to the room.

The homeowners now are set for gracious entertaining. Her work as an artist influenced their choice of soft, white satin-finished cabinets, rich granite countertops, warm wood floors and a pomegranate/sage green palette in the drapery treatments. ◆

THE BEST OF SIGNATURE KITCHENS 133

Photographer: Bill Busch

A snack center is tucked behind the refrigerator.

country elegance

When this Long Island family built a new home, their dream kitchen came along with it. The refined classic country look found throughout the home was matched in the kitchen. Together with its good looks, the room is loaded with functionality—perfectly suited to the family of five and easily accommodating the mother's love of cooking and penchant for entertaining. The clients' wish list for this new kitchen included an abundance of counter space, plenty of storage areas, state-of-the-art equipment and knock 'em dead aesthetics. Certified Kitchen Designer Don Boico of Classic Kitchen & Bath Center Ltd. made some changes to the original plan to ensure that all those needs were met.

Providing enough space for cooking and entertaining was a priority, so an eating area was moved to an adjacent space, allowing more room for cabinetry, counters and an oversized island. Generous workspaces by the range and refrigerator ease tasks. The large work island provides even more counter space and doubles as a buffet.

Storage abounds in wall and base cabinets, as well as the island perimeter. Glass-fronted double wall cabinets contribute to the country flair and display collectibles.

Top-of-the-line appliances from Bosch, Sub-Zero and Viking make meal preparation a pleasure. A small (6 by 10 feet) space behind the refrigerator wall is designed as a snack center and includes a microwave. This room, reminiscent of a butler's pantry, makes a convenient but out-of-the-way place to make snacks and sandwiches—and offers even more storage space. Cabinetry and counters match those in the kitchen proper.

The beadboard walls and ceiling, farmhouse sink, pot rack and glass-front cabinets contribute to the country elegance of the room. The custom wood floor brings warmth and beauty with a strong design statement. Three-dimensional wall tiles, crown molding and pewter cabinet hardware are perfect finishing touches to this dream kitchen. ◆

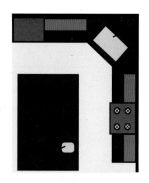

Special Features:
Custom wood floor, spacious island that doubles as buffet, corbels beneath wall cabinets and turned columns on island and sinkbase cabinet give "furniture" feel; stacked wall cabinets with glass-front doors

Dimensions:
30 feet x 17 feet

Products Used:
Cabinetry: Private Label; Flooring: Custom Hardwood; Countertops: Granite; Sinks: Franke stainless steel on island, Whitehaus farm sink; Faucets: Franke; Dishwasher: Bosch; Range: Viking; Refrigerator: Sub-Zero

DESIGNER

Don Boico, CKD, CR
Classic Kitchen & Bath
Center, Ltd.;
locations at 1062
Northern Blvd.,
Roslyn, NY 11576,
516/621-7700
and 60 B Jobs Lane,
Southampton, NY
11968;
631/204-9500

DESIGNER

Chaim Sharon,
Kuche+Cucina, 489
Route 17 South,
Paramus, NJ 07652;
201/261-5221

Silvery steel, a splash of cobalt blue.

a contemporary blend

Special Features:
Wall paneling system with glass shelves; very rare Blue Bahia Granite

Dimensions:
16 feet x 9 feet

Products Used:
Cabinets: SieMatic 7007BR; Undercabinet Lighting, Backsplash Accessories and Glass Shelf Systems: SieMatic; Countertops: Blue Bahia Granite; Sink(s): Franke; Oven and Cooktop: Miele; Dishwasher, Washer/Dryer: Miele

When a New Jersey couple moved into their waterfront apartment overlooking the skyline of Manhattan, they took one look at the kitchen and knew it had to be completely redesigned.

Rather than being set apart, the kitchen was open into the dining and living areas. It had to blend, to become an integral part of the beautifully decorated contemporary space.

The homeowners wanted a built-in "furniture-like" look. They turned to Kuche+Cucina for solutions, and designer Chaim Sharon got down to work. Beginning with placement, Sharon created a work area on one side of the kitchen, treating the other side as the connecting element between the kitchen, dining area and living room.

Because the kitchen is so visible from other areas, Sharon blended it skillfully by covering the refrigerator, washer/dryer and dishwasher in wood panels. He placed wood panels as a backsplash as well, which merges into a paneling system with glass shelving near the dining area.

SieMatic maple cabinetry was chosen for its clean lines, then sparked with lots of oversized steel handles and steel toe kicks. Other steel elements are found throughout the kitchen, including the stainless undercabinet light fixtures that support different wall fittings and accessories. The "silverish, no-color-like" aspect of the stainless steel proved the perfect counterpoint to the warmth of the cabinets.

One bold stroke remained: Sharon splashed vivid cobalt blue across the composition with the exotic Blue Bahia Granite countertops.◆

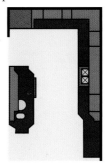

Photographer: Michael Kaskel

From dark to dramatic.

asian influence

The homeowners were clear and specific in what they wanted: more natural light and a clean, modern look with a touch of Asian influence. It would take an incredible transformation. For the kitchen was dark and cramped and presented a real challenge to designer David M. McNulty of Kitchen & Bath Creations, Inc.

After consultations, brainstorming and soul-searching, a bold and imaginative plan was made.

Removing the wall between the kitchen and the dining room resulted in a grander space within which to work the transformation. All the existing windows were retained and a large skylight was added. A flared ceiling, allowing more space for beams of light to penetrate, is a subtle but masterful touch.

Next, carefully angled work areas were created that allow a panoramic view of the home.

A second oven was required, and that prompted the designer to mix microwave with convection and place it ergonomically in the pantry cabinet. A small sitting area behind a multilevel peninsula offers the perfect spot for entertaining guests. To accent and enhance the newly found natural light, specially placed recessed niches hold personal momentos and decorative pieces illuminated with puck lights. Frosted glass on two cabinet doors creates a focal point for the kitchen, while softening the movement of horizontal and vertical lines.

The transformation was complete. The kitchen is now the heart of the home: a serene and enchanting place to gather.◆

Special Features:
Multilevel countertops, multicolor slate backsplash, recessed illuminated niches

Dimensions:
19 feet x 10 feet

Products Used:
Cabinetry: Holiday IDC Series; Flooring: Wood; Countertops: Granite; Sink(s): Franke; Faucets: KWC; Dishwasher: Bosch; Range: Dacor; Hood: Best; Lighting: Alkco; Refrigerator: GE; Wallcovering: Slate backsplash

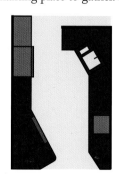

DESIGNER

David M. McNulty, CKD, Kitchen & Bath Creations, Inc., 604 Devon Ave., Park Ridge, IL 60068; 847/696-1860

Photographer: Robert Torento

A green granite island provides a lovely focal point.

homework today,
entertaining tonight

When Phil and Jean Shapiro decided to remodel their traditional-style New England home, they knew just whom to turn to. They had seen designer Paul Rossini's work at the Boston Junior League show house in Westwood, Massachusetts. There was no question that he was the right man for the job.

"The Shapiros wanted to create a homey, warm atmosphere where their two daughters could be comfortable doing their homework, yet elegant and formal enough for entertaining company," says Rossini. "Planning was key to be sure that the finished space would allow optimal flow and comfort for its mixed uses."

The old kitchen area was combined with an existing unheated sunporch to create the dream room. Two-zone radiant heat was installed. The family could easily walk around barefoot on the chilliest New England winter day.

To unify the space, Rossini raised an existing sliding door 8 inches. The homeowners agreed to transposing the former living and dining rooms, optimizing the flow between the kitchen and the dining room with a 5-foot opening cut between the two. One important requirement of the job was creating a mud room. This area is outfitted with cubbies for the children's backpacks and a storage bench. Now the family can sit comfortably while removing shoes or boots, then toss them neatly out of sight.

Some features that make this kitchen special include nose and cove doors with brown glaze and a complementary green-stained island. Honed green Hawaiian granite tops the island, designed to look like a freestanding piece of furniture. The ceiling boasts handsome beams that Rossini fashioned from old recycled roof rafters.

Associate designer Diane Silverman worked closely with Mrs. Shapiro to coordinate the materials so the colors and textures would harmonize. Silverman also suggested accessories to pull the whole project together.

Says Jean Shapiro: "I'm thrilled with everything! It's even more beautiful than I could have hoped for." ◆

Special Features:
Glazed maple cabinets accented by a contrasting green island assembly that has been heavily distressed and capped with honed green Hawaiian granite

Dimensions:
17 feet x 14.5 feet

Products Used:
Cabinetry: Millbrook;
Sink(s): Whitehaus;
Faucets: Whitehaus;
Drawer Pulls: Topknobs

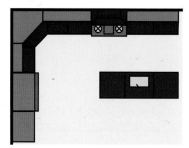

DESIGNER

Paul Rossini, Kitchens
Etc., 221 Worcester
Road, Framingham,
MA 01701;
508/879-3377

DESIGNER

Ellen A. Shelly,
Shelly Design, Inc.,
P. O. Box 97,
Batavia, OH 45103;
513/752-1606

the aesthetics of
symmetry

Tim Grondin Photography

The cabinet had to be multifunctional and beautiful.

Special Features:
Two dishwashers to right of sink for loading and unloading dishes from eating area, Custom Sub-Zero bar wine cooler in decorative hutch, single-level counters for clean open look, gathering and dining area well outside the work area

Dimensions:
20 feet x 20 feet

Products Used:
Cabinetry: WoodMode; Countertops: Granite; Sink(s): Kohler; Dishwasher: ASKO; Cooktop, Hood and Oven: Thermador; Refrigerator: Sub-Zero; Cabinet Hardware: Cliffside; Wine storage: Sub-Zero; Flooring: maple hardwood; Lighting: recessed can

New or remodel? As an active professional couple, these homeowners wanted to come home to an environment that was warm, inviting and relaxing. They also wanted a no-nonsense efficient working space. After consulting with designer Ellen A. Shelly of Shelly Design, Inc., they decided on the increasingly popular great room concept.

Key to the space was to be a furniture piece at the end of the kitchen. This cabinet had to function as a decorative area to display dishes and crystal, to hold cookbooks and to disguise a bar area. The homeowners are interested in the aesthetics of symmetry, so the first challenge was to design a furniture-like piece that was visually balanced and met all the criteria specified. In order for the piece to function as furniture, it had to stand on its own. This was accomplished with color, as Vintage White was introduced into the kitchen.

For warmth and added detail, the other cabinetry chosen was a medium-toned maple (WoodMode, Beacon Hill Door Profile). With the desired symmetry and visual appeal in place, Ellen's next challenge was how to incorporate a television set into the kitchen. It should be visible from all areas without becoming a focal point.

This she accomplished by putting the microwave into the corner and designing a custom cabinet that could also house the television. Decorative details tie the furniture piece to the custom cabinet. Placing the commercial range to the right of the corner achieved a suitable focal point.

The third and final challenge was to develop a table and secondary work island. The couple's cooking habits dictated a countertop opposite the range. This would enable them to remove items from both the main and secondary ovens with an immediate drop zone to save additional movement. This was accomplished by designing a single-level work surface with a table at one end that did not interfere with the work triangle.

Now the homeowners have a functional, beautiful kitchen—a fine haven to come home to. ◆

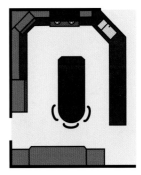

Photographer: Christopher Covey

A hand-trawled custom hood over the cooktop creates an interesting focal point.

from so-so
to bellisimo

Breaking up the boxy look of the kitchen was the goal on this project. By removing the peninsula, the new layout opened the kitchen to the adjacent family room, providing a family eating area at the end of a storage-loaded island.

The flavor of the room is Old World Tuscany, influenced by the client's strong Italian heritage. Distressed country French style maple doors with a keepsake finish help establish a warm, nostalgic look. A very special backsplash complements granite countertops. The hand-trawled custom hood, trimmed with lovely Walker & Zanger stone liners, created a beautiful focal point. Additional items of interest are the pass-through bay window and display cabinets with Queen Ann mullion doors. The lighting was updated from an existing recessed fluorescent ceiling to halogen down lights with halogen track lights installed under the wall cabinets.

This beautiful kitchen is the result of two design professionals working together to provide their client with the best possible advice to make her dream come true. While David Johnson, CKD, worked with the client to create the kitchen design and resolve the lighting and mechanical problems, Pamela Denson advised the client on her choice of countertop, tile backsplash and all of the aesthetic elements so important in creating just the right look and feel.◆

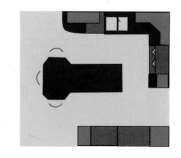

Special Features:
Crystal Cabinets frameless cabinets with 3/4-inch clear maple drawer boxes and full extension undermount guides; maple doors in country French style with Salem stain, distressing, wearing and Van Dyke highlight; halogen under-cabinet track lights; custom hand-trawled hood with Walker & Zanger stone liners; two cabinets with Queen Ann mullion doors and lighted interiors; large island with loads of storage and seating for three.

Dimensions:
15' x 13'

Products Used:
Cabinetry: Crystal Cabinet Works
Flooring: Hardwood
Countertops: Granite
Sink(s): Kohler
Faucets: Grohe
Dishwasher: KitchenAid
Cooktop: KitchenAid
Refrigerator: KitchenAid
Oven: KitchenAid
Hood: ModernAire
Pulls: Hafele

DESIGNER

David W. Johnson, CKD
Better Kitchens & Baths Inc.
1884 Eastman Ave., #106
Ventura, CA 93003
805-644-5844
betterkitchens-baths.com

DESIGNER

Annette Pierce
Bouchard-Pierce
127 Pearl St.
Essex Junction, VT 05452
802-878-4822

Photographer: Carolyn L. Bates

A built-in desk
is an elegant
but functional
work space.

fit for a
(coo)king

Special Features:
Commercial cooktop;
pot-filler faucet; farm-
style sink; tile backsplash;
double refrigerator;
warming oven; desk in
kitchen

Dimensions:
17' x 18.5'

Products Used:
Cabinetry: Cabinets by
Nichols
Countertops: Hillside
Stone Products, Baltic
Brown granite
Sink(s): Whitehaus
Faucets: Whitehaus
Dishwasher: KitchenAid
Cooktop: KitchenAid
Refrigerator: KitchenAid
Wallcovering: Best Tile
Oven: KitchenAid
Hood: KitchenAid
Microwave: GE
Mouldings: Raymond
Enkeboll Designs

Part of an approximately 4,200-square-foot home, this new kitchen project stood apart from the rest of the traditionally styled and decorated home in look and feel. The clients were a young couple with three pre-teen boys who needed a larger space with a kitchen that would please even a professional chef, as the husband of the family is quite the cook.

Designer Annette Pierce of Bouchard-Pierce in Vermont was familiar with the family's lifestyle and tastes from a previous kitchen she had done for them. Though they had a very informal lifestyle, they preferred a kitchen with a more formal feel and had determined that a French Country look is one they both really liked. Pierce achieved this by using beaded board, custom decorative mouldings with a carved grape motif and a sanded toffee glaze, which lent to the Old World look.

The unusually shaped room's multiple wall angles made placement of appliances a challenge. The two large refrigerators were positioned where access was best and integrity of the overall look was least compromised. On either side of the commercial cooktop are pull-out spice racks. Across the room, a warming drawer is located below the double wall oven. The island includes room for three to snack or study, as well as a large workspace and oversize drawers for storing pots, pans and mixing bowls.

The result is a kitchen suited for royalty.◆

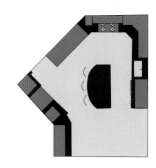

Photographer: Steve Whitsitt

Interesting use
of lighting
adds warmth
and drama.

window
wonderland

A secluded hillside property with a commanding view of Vermont's Green Mountains is the setting for this newly constructed contemporary farmhouse. The building plans called for the living and dining areas of the home to be open to the kitchen, which has numerous windows facing the beautiful vistas. The homeowners desired an efficient kitchen space that added character to the adjoining rooms.

The windows, located on three of the kitchen walls, created the biggest challenge for Designer Matt Grundy of Builder Specialties. Due to the limited wall space available within the kitchen, Grundy and the homeowners decided to house the refrigerator, as well as most of the bulk storage, in a large pantry adjacent to the kitchen. The wall space was dedicated to storing glass and dishware in cabinets with furniture effects and mullion glass doors, which create interesting and functional storage.

To give the kitchen a farmhouse look, Grundy chose also to use painted cabinetry with inset beaded panel doors. Warm cherry floors, a cathedral ceiling, antique green painted walls and solid granite countertops combine with arched openings and painted columns to create a casually elegant feeling within the space. The combination of natural materials and an abundance of natural light provides this family with a relaxing atmosphere to enjoy with friends and each other.◆

Special Features:
Dual undercounter ovens; dropped baking area; raised corner shelves in matching granite

Dimensions:
15' x 12'

Products Used:
Cabinetry: Norwood Custom
Flooring: Cherry
Countertops: Laurentian granite
Sink(s): Kindred stainless steel
Cooktop: Dacor
Refrigerator: Sub-Zero
Oven: Jenn-Air

DESIGNER

Matt Grundy
Builder Specialties Inc.
92 River St., Suite 1
Montpelier, VT 05602
802-223-5583

DESIGNER

Nancy Joseph
The Cabinet Tree
8602 Farmington Blvd.
Suite 1
Germantown, TN 38139
901.309.1887

A ceiling-height integrated island houses the refrigerator.

fantasy
island

Special Features:
Ceiling-height integrated island, housing refrigerator; cooking grotto with pot-filler faucet; Unique design features include cabinet finished trim at window; "boot" table top

Dimensions:
19' x 15'5"

Products Used:
Cabinetry: Custom Cupboards
Flooring: Elm hardwood
Countertops: Tropical Brown 3CM granite
Sink(s): Whitehaus
Faucets: Whitehaus
Dishwasher: Bosch
Cooktop: Bosch
Lighting: Task, recessed, stained glass
Refrigerator: GE Monogram
Wallcovering: Tequila
Oven: Bosch

"Heather" was a million-dollar new construction project, and the builder asked the question every designer loves to hear: What do you think?

Design liberty was given to The Cabinet Tree, Collierville, Tenn., to create a totally new look. That challenge had designers re-thinking their approach to an island. An exceptional area to emphasize detail, designers opted to make it the focus of their attention.

Once the criteria was identified, it launched distinctive, creative options into the plan. For example, the built-in refrigerator was to become the back wall for the ceiling-height island. The warmth of wood wraps entirely around the island to create an additional opportunity for design. Beaded wood walls and a pair of mantels reflect unique and unexpected detail. The "boot" extension table top provides exceptional storage and seating.

As the 'frig found its home right in the middle of the kitchen, designers were able to achieve a four-zoned area. The main

sink, breakfast bar, cooking grotto and prep area are designated locations that the gourmet or hands-on family can appreciate.

A few finishing touches completed the kitchen. The Cabinet Tree chose to integrate and design a trim detail at the main sink. The window is wrapped in the same Irish cream finish as the cabinets. Some furniture detail concluded the specifics of the design. Tropical brown granite, rusted iron hardware, wall-mounted faucetry and Tiffany pendants contributed to the project's great success.◆

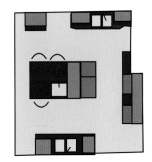

Carved onlays
on cabinets and
the range hood
create texture
and character.

long island
special

The challenge presented to Classic Kitchen & Bath Center's design team led by Fara Boico was to provide a functional and beautiful country kitchen for this Long Island homeowner. As always, Classic Kitchen's design philosophy is form follows function, and all throughout this space, this was paramount. A work center with more than adequate counter space next to each appliance and an easily accessible clean-up center in the island are just a few of the items that demonstrate the firm's commitment to functionality.

But man cannot live on function alone, and Classic Kitchen places a premium on aesthetic beauty, as well. This is apparent in the use of egg-and-dart moulding, pull-out fluted columns for storage, and glass doors in an extra-deep center cabinet. A pair of carved corbels accented with a carved onlay support the wood range hood. A Sub-Zero refrigerator and freezer are in keeping with

the furniture look throughout the kitchen.

The perimeter of the room is finished in a mocha cream glaze on birch with a 25 percent low sheen. As a complement, the island was done in a tavern green on cherry finish. The countertops were done in ivory chiffon granite, offset with Paveo green granite on the island.

In all, the design team met the desires of this homeowner to create a functional and spectacularly beautiful kitchen.◆

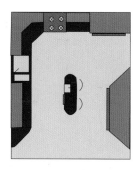

Special Features:
Carved onlays; small island with corbels; pull-out fluted columns for storage; all beveled glass; individual Lite wall cabinets; egg-and-dart moulding on doors and inset into crown moulding

Dimensions:
24' x 11'

Products Used:
Cabinetry: Custom Cabinetry
Flooring: Oak
Countertops: Granite
Sink(s): Franke
Faucets: Franke
Dishwasher: Gaggenau
Cooktop: Bosch
Refrigerator: Sub-Zero
Oven: Thermador

DESIGNER

Fara Boico
Classic Kitchen & Bath
Center Ltd.
1062 Northern Blvd.
Roslyn, NY 11576
516-621-7700

DESIGNER

Cindy Carbone
Curtis Kitchen & Bath
Center
1 Webb St.
Danvers, MA 01923
978-777-0890

Photographer: David Pratt

Full oak overlay cabinets replaced painted white cabinets.

shaker
sensation

Special Features:
Wine rack with stem holder; trash compactor in island; full overlay oak shaker-style cabinets to match homeowners' furniture

Dimensions:
13.5' X 13'

Products Used:
Cabinetry: Candlelight Cabinetry
Flooring: Natural Oak
Countertops: Corian in Cobalt Blue
Sink(s): Whitehaus Collection
Faucets: Whitehaus Collection
Dishwasher: Maytag
Stove: GE
Refrigerator: GE
Wallcovering: Paint
Backsplash: Antigua Tile
Compactor: GE
Hardware: Whitehaus Collection

Revitalizing a typical 1960's kitchen with little wall space was a challenge for Designer Cindy Carbone. Creating a contemporary shaker style to match the homeowners' existing furnishings and coordinating with the existing hardwood flooring were the main objectives of this remodeling job of a Hamilton, Mass., home. Previously this home had undergone several remodels from its original split-entry design, including removing walls between the kitchen and dining room.

The homeowners requested that the old New England-style pine cabinets, long ago painted white, be updated. Carbone chose full oak overlay shaker-style cabinets, which have lots of built-in features, such as rolling shelves, as well as tray and cutlery dividers. The owners' love of wine prompted the desire for a built-in wine rack and stem holder. Tall cabinetry houses a broom closet and pantry.

An octagon-shaped island replaced a rectangular island, bringing angles into the L-shaped room for a bit more interest. The new island features ample space for food preparation and provides a gathering spot for children to do homework or have a snack. It also houses a trash compactor and angled cabinetry, which provide ample storage.

Cobalt blue Corian countertops and an undermount sink make clean-up a snap. A coordinating Antigua tile backsplash completes the look of this new kitchen that better fits the family's more contemporary lifestyle.◆

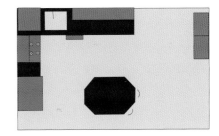

DESIGNER

Linda Sciarra, CKD, and
Lina Inacio
Fresh Impressions Inc.
326 Route 22
Green Brook, NJ 08812
732-424-2200

Staggered cabinet heights provide secondary focal points.

mass
appeal

Special Features:
Custom hood; fluted columns; Enkebol appliqués; tumbled marble mosaic backsplash; staggered cabinet heights

Dimensions:
15' x 14'

Products Used:
Cabinetry: Cuisine Cabico
Flooring: Ceramic tile
Countertops: UBA Tuba granite
Sink(s): Elkay
Dishwashers: Asko
Range: Viking
Refrigerator: Sub-Zero
Warming Drawer: Viking

Designing a kitchen for a spec house presents a unique set of challenges. When a designer has a specific client, he or she will generally try to create something very personal for that client, taking into consideration the client's lifestyle and individual tastes to design a space that best suits his or her needs. In a spec house, a designer is creating for the unknown. The job calls for elements rich in drama yet versatile enough to appeal to every potential homebuyer.

Working with Lina Inacio and designing to please the masses as opposed to fulfilling specific requests, Certified Kitchen Designer Linda Sciarra of Fresh Impressions Inc. set about to create a spectacular kitchen for what was to be a large and elegant home. She decided to make the kitchen's main focal point the cooking area. By placing it in a corner and giving it a spectacular mantel-style hood that reaches all the way to the high ceilings, she did just that. Incorporating carved corbels,

appliqués on the face of the hood and moulding details, she was able to create a very decorative focal point. Everything else in the room—mini-corbels, fluted columns, the angled corners on the island and cabinets—reflected what was done in that corner without overpowering it.

The house is no longer a spec house, but rather home to one lucky New Jersey family. It goes without saying that its kitchen helped close the sale.◆

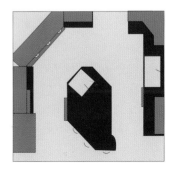

Photographer: Mike Teipen, CMKD

Varying surface
textures and
colors create
drama.

old meets
new

The newly constructed home was to be in a Village of Dreams tour, which otherwise included homes built in the 19th century. The client/builder took period style to the maximum, creating an Italianate home while considering every detail for authenticity.

The kitchen was small in comparison to the rest of the home. While maintaining a look and feel of warmth, it also needed a touch of elegance. Therefore, the designers left the corners of the room open, allowing space to hang a sconce or picture. An entire wall was used to create a special hutch. To achieve contemporary lighting for tasks and ambiance, the designer used under-cabinet halogens and an antique chandelier above the island.

A local craftsman built a mahogany furniture piece with many rollouts. Open cabinets were designed to mimic the architecture of the arched doors throughout the house. An artisan hand-painted and glazed the unfinished cabinetry to

achieve a special look and color.

The butler's pantry, which holds a wine cooler and copper sink, separates the dining room from the kitchen. Mullion doors with mouth-blown glass were used in this area to match windows throughout the home.

Overall, the design accomplished the warm, yet elegant, Italianate look the builder wanted to achieve, and exceeded all expectations for a beautiful kitchen.◆

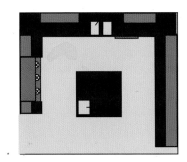

Special Features:
Cabinetry finish by Renaissance Finishes by Kathleen O'Neil Stevens; stunning tile backsplash; custom mahogany stereo center; European pewter finish hardware

Dimensions:
15' x 15'
5' x 15' (Butler's pantry)

Products Used:
Cabinetry: Teipen Signature Cabinetry
Flooring: Santos Mahogany
Countertops: Tan brown granite and solid mahogany on island
Sink(s): Kohler
Faucets: Concinnity
Dishwasher: Viking
Range: Viking
Lighting: Antique chandelier
Refrigerator: Viking
Wallcovering: Renaissance Finishes by Kathleen O'Neil Stevens
Warming Drawer: Viking

DESIGNER

Kristen Zwitt and
Mike Teipen, CMKBD
Kitchens by Teipen, Inc.
1035 N. State Rd. 135
Greenwood, IN 46142
317-888-7345

DESIGNER

Chaim Sharon
Kuche-Cucina
489 Rt. 17 S.
Paramus, NJ 07652
201-261-5221

Photographer: Mark S. Cunningham

Stainless appliances with anegre colored wood provide dramatic contrast.

european
update

Special Features:
Contemporary styling with a definite European sense of sophistication and function

Dimensions:
16' x 11'

Products Used:
Cabinetry: SC16 Anegre by SieMatic
Flooring: Wood with granite accents
Countertops: Seaweed granite
Sink: Franke
Faucets: Grohe
Dishwasher: Miele
Lighting: Low-voltage halogen
Refrigerator: Sub-Zero
Wallcovering: SieMatic wall panel system
Oven: Thermador commercial-style range
Microwave: GE Monogram

Though it wasn't as old as it looked, prior to remodeling, the kitchen of this Suffern, N.Y., home looked tired and dated, and its low-quality components were showing serious wear and tear. The homeowners called for a total makeover, so the area was completely redesigned with modern styling.

The clients didn't have a lengthy wish list, but knew they wanted an airy open space with contemporary European ambiance that blended with their dining area. Using a highly unusual and dramatic anegre color, a yellow-white to pinkish brown color derived from a wood grown in Central Africa, as well as lots of stainless steel and glass, achieved the sophisticated look.

Often, designers load every available wall with cabinets, but Chaim Sharon of Kuche-Cucina opted for the chic and innovative SieMatic wall paneling sys-

tem on both sides of the kitchen. One side features open shelves. The main wall, where the range is located, has sleek stacked glass-door cabinets on either side. The contrast against a full-height granite backsplash is dramatic. Maple hardwood floors are accented with three granite squares. A stainless steel range hood and stainless steel toe kicks beautifully complement the cabinet doors, base cabinets and floors. Low voltage halogen fixtures provide a subtle warm glow, enhancing the natural light streaming through triple window panels.◆

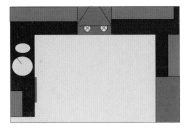

DESIGNER

Reidar Klemetsen
Nordic Kitchens and
Baths
4437 Veterans Blvd.
Metairie, LA 70006
504-888-2300

Photographer: Richard Vallon

Showcasing fine china and crystal was a priority for the homeowners.

appliances
in abundance

Special Features:
Raised bar area with seating for up to six; display cabinet with glass doors for collectibles; TV cabinet

Dimensions:
17' x 16'

Products Used:
Cabinetry: Fieldstone
Countertops: Mariposa Green granite
Sink(s): Franke
Faucets: Franke
Dishwasher: Bosch
Cooktop: Gaggenau
Refrigerator: Sub-Zero
Wallcovering: Painted Sheetrock
Oven: Viking

The homeowners were looking forward to lots of entertaining in their new home, and their specific request for their kitchen was lots of appliances, which they needed on hand to create culinary masterpieces for their guests. The challenge for Designer Reidar Klemetsen was to fill the kitchen space with appliances of all shapes and sizes, yet keep the area uncrowded and inviting. Plenty of storage space—corner cabinets, pull-out drawers and roll-out shelves—for appliances used only occasionally was the solution.

Anticipated appliance usage also prompted Klemetsen to carefully consider outlet placement: No need for cooks to have to relocate small appliances in order to use them.

In addition to the typical kitchen appliances, the homeowners wanted a television on top of their oven cabinets. The challenge here was keeping the ovens the proper distance from the floor and the TV at a viewable height. The top of the cabinet was lopped off to accomplish

this. One corner was left open so family members can watch TV from the six-person seating area.

To showcase the family's fine china and crystal, a cabinet with glass doors was installed next to the refrigerator. Wall cabinets between the two kitchen windows also have glass doors.

The result of this fairly straightforward project is a kitchen the homeowners and their guests will enjoy for years to come.◆

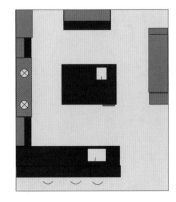

Photographer: David D. Livingston

Upper cabinet
doors have
textured frosted
glass that
provides
extraordinary
architectural
detail.

bachelor-pad
posh

This kitchen was designed for a young, single stockbroker, who had recently purchased a New York City penthouse condominium and wanted to renovate to suit his needs and personal tastes. The client does much cooking and entertaining, thus he needed a professional kitchen with full-size appliances, which provided quite a challenge for the designers, as the space allocated for the kitchen was unusually small. In addition, the room has varying ceiling heights and minimal storage. Therefore, it did not function ergonomically.

In order to best utilize the space, the cabinet and appliance portion of the kitchen was designed as an L-shape. Incorporated into this space are an under-counter oven with two 12-inch cooktops above and a 22-inch sink with garbage disposal. In order to create more storage space, designers installed a second row of cabinets above the customary wall cabinets in areas where the ceiling was higher. On the opposite

wall, they placed a narrow countertop with a shallow icemaker and microwave, which allows for more workspace. Designers also enlarged a small alcove to accommodate a narrow refrigerator and then pulled the unit off the wall to add a shallow pantry.

A combination of materials, executive stained cherry wood; frosted glass; stainless steel appliances; black granite countertops, floors and backsplashes; and aluminum handles, combine to give this bachelor's kitchen a rich, sophisticated look and feel.◆

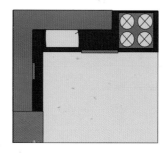

Special Features:
Double row of wall cabinets to utilize varying ceiling heights; textured frosted glass door inserts

Dimensions:
8' x 7'

Products Used:
Cabinetry: Regency Kitchens
Flooring: Black Absoluto granite, International Stone & Accessories
Countertops: Black Absoluto granite, International Stone & Accessories
Sink(s): Franke
Faucets: Franke
Dishwasher: Miele
Cooktop: Miele
Lighting: Juno
Refrigerator: Sub-Zero
Oven: Miele
Icemaker: U-Lin

DESIGNER

Rochelle Kalisch, CKD
Regency Kitchens
4204 14th Ave.
Brooklyn, NY 11219
718-435-4266

204E. 77th Street
New York City, NY 10021
212.517.8707

DESIGNER

Barbara Terkildsen
Barbara Terkildsen
Interiors, LLC
32 Bradley Lane
Sandy Hook, CT 06482
203.426.4223
www.btkitchens.com

Crown moulding enhances the custom maple and white painted cabinets.

new york
retreat

Special Features:
Custom color on wood cabinets, Kirkstone countertops, hand-painted tiles, custom glass, skylights, high ceiling above sink side of kitchen, lighting directed at ceiling

Dimensions:
17' x 30'

Products Used:
Cabinetry: Custom
Flooring: Wide Plank Oak
Countertops: Kirkstone
Sink(s): Stainless
Faucets: KWC Brushed Nickel
Dishwasher: ASKO
Cooktop: 48" Wolf
Lighting: Holt Kotter
Refrigerator: Sub-Zero
Wallcovering: Paint, Benjamin Moore
Hood: Best Hood
Trash Compactor: KitchenAid Microwave: KitchenAid

When this high-powered New York City couple bought their weekend home on a New York lake, they immediately called Barbara Terkildsen and asked her to work with them on yet another project. With the unified efforts of Terkildsen's creative talents and the homeowners' vision, they knew the end result would be the desired combination of design and sophistication.

Since they spend most of their weekends in the country, the homeowners envisioned a large kitchen where comfort and country elegance would be waiting for them, a place for entertaining friends and family. The project began with the construction of a new wing, which included the kitchen, pool, morning room and master bath.

The kitchen was designed with windows around the dining area overlooking the lake, and custom banquettes were built beneath the windows. High-angled ceilings with skylights and ambient lighting were incorporated to enhance the work and dining areas of the kitchen. Undercabinet lighting was also included in the design

of the kitchen. Because the clients are tall, the height of the base cabinets was elevated, and the stove was raised off the floor.

Custom maple wood cabinets and white painted cabinets were enhanced with crown molding detail. Hammered glass was special ordered for the wall cabinets, and a 54" stainless-steel hood was situated above the 48" stove and hand-painted tile backsplash. Accessories include a plate drawer, recycling cabinet, pantry, bread drawer and a display cabinet for the customers' Yellow Ware. The homeowners' classic American country furnishings and art were the perfect finish to this luxurious kitchen design.◆

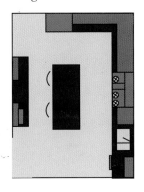

PHOTOGRAPHER: OLSON PHOTOGRAPHIC, LLC

This distinctive kitchen was inspired by antique ships.

nautically inspired

Betsy House of Kitchen & Bath Designs, LLC combined efforts with designer/builder Hayward H. Gatch to craft this stately kitchen with a focus on the client's love for antique ships. When designers suggested a yacht-style kitchen complete with unique design elements and breathtaking ocean view, this home-owner eagerly jumped on board.

After purchasing this oceanfront property complete with a spectacular view of a secluded lighthouse, the homeowner decided to fully remodel the home. This distinctive custom galley was the result. An inviting banquette, chamfered posts and a paneled soffit successfully mirror the small cozy spaces characteristic of a boat, while the lighted teak grating on the floor and the "hatch" above offer the illusion of being between the decks of a ship. The white walls and pale green accents create a blended motif and dignified elegance.

While creating a kitchen worthy of a yacht galley was a challenge in itself, the designers also faced the challenge of adding functionality and comfort to entertain friends and family. The homeowner desired an accessible space with the option of closing it off to the dining room when serving guests. This was cleverly and stylishly achieved by adding glass display cabinets and mahogany swinging doors. Altogether, this kitchen, as it reflects the character of its owner and provides an enjoyable cooking space for the gathering of family and friends, can be described as nothing less than a nautical masterpiece.◆

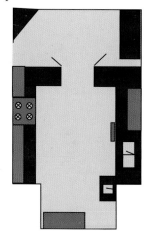

Special Features:
Furniture "feet" on cabinetry; antique heart pine countertops; hand-painted local fish on tiles; ship's lanterns; custom hood; message center; banquette

Dimensions:
12' x 27'

Products Used:
Cabinetry: Custom by Deschenes & Cooper Architectural Millwork
Flooring: Antique heart pine w/ teak grating
Countertops: Antique heart pine with marine finish
Sink(s): Franke stainless steel
Faucets: Franke Triflow
Dishwasher: Asko
Stove: Viking 48" stainless steel
Lighting: W.A.C. Halogen
Refrigerator: Sub-Zero
Wallcovering: Painted brick-cut terra cotta tiles
Hood: Custom wood hood w/ stainless steel liner

DESIGNER

Betsy House
Kitchen & Bath Designs,
LLC by Betsy House
11 Heritage Drive
Stonington, CT 06378
860.535.4982

Stainless steel appliances are softened by a decorative backsplash.

functional elegance

Don Boico of Classic Kitchen and Bath Center, Ltd. had the classic "form follows function" philosophy in mind when he designed the remodel for this elegant kitchen. While improving the function of the space with reconstructed work zones, the designer was able to fit the new kitchen neatly into the original floorplan.

The homeowners desired space enough for entertaining large groups of friends and family, all the while keeping a cozy atmosphere for smaller, more intimate gatherings. Classic Kitchen and Bath managed this by incorporating open counterspaces into the design, and by constructing a new breakfast bar for additional seating. The space was further utilized by installing a corner sink to provide a more spacious work surface. All these additions were constructed without an expansion so as to use only the existing space.

The sleek lines of the stainless-steel appliances were softened by a decorative backsplash and custom-embellished hood. The white Neff cabinets are enhanced by the pale granite countertops, and the creamy cabinetry is accentuated by decorative egg-and-dart molding, turned legs and glass mullion doors. Beautiful hardwood floors provide the final touch for this timeless kitchen. The end result is a beautiful space that serves as a fully functional culinary workspace and an inviting venue for entertaining. ◆

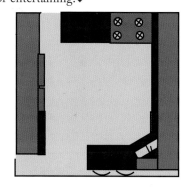

Special Features:
Buttercream glaze finish; layout follows the philosophy of "form follows function"

Dimensions:
18' x 15'

Products Used:
Cabinetry: Neff
Flooring: Hardwood
Countertops: Granite
Dishwasher: Asko
Range: Wolf
Refrigerator: Sub-Zero

DESIGNER

Don Boico, CKD, CR
Classic Kitchen and Bath
Center, Ltd.
1062 Northern Blvd.
Roslyn, NY 11576
516.621.7700

PHOTOGRAPHER: STEVE WHITSITT

The removal
of a wall and
the installation
of a window
dramatically
enlarged
the space.

dream
kitchen

This active suburban Philadelphia family longed for more space and an updated design for their 1970's-era kitchen. Desiring such, they contacted Salvatore Manzo of Renaissance to help them plan a space large enough for entertaining, but intimate enough for family meals.

The renovation began by removing the wall between the kitchen and dining room. A large window was installed above the sink, and the eating area was enlarged with the addition of French doors to increase the space and capture the breathtaking view of the adjacent pond.

Warm maple beaded inset cabinets finished with an olive glaze were chosen for the cabinetry. Custom wall cabinets with olive paint and hand-distressed glass doors were also added. To accommodate the needs of the family cook, Manzo designed space for a commercial stove, custom hood, warming drawer and fully integrated dishwasher. A second sink was added to the island for food prep and quick drinks for the children.

For easy maintenance, honed quartz counter surfacing was installed throughout the kitchen. Recessed lighting was used around the cabinet perimeter, stainless steel under-cabinet lighting for the cooking area, and two pendants with decorative lampshades were added to the island. Crackled hand-cast brick shaped tiles completed the cooking area. An oak floor with a rich mocha stain served as the finishing touch. The result is a spacious kitchen with a trendy design.◆

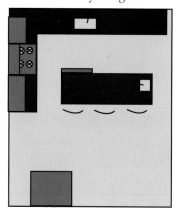

Special Features:
"Shaker-legged" island; custom stainless hood; glazed beaded inset base cabinetry; painted distressed upper cabinetry; crackled brick tile backsplash

Dimensions:
26' x 17'

Products Used:
Cabinetry: Elmwood
Flooring: Oak hardwood
Countertops: CaesarStone
Sink(s): Kindred
Faucets: Aquadis
Dishwasher: Meile
Stove: KitchenAid
Refrigerator: KitchenAid
Microwave: GE
Warming drawer: KitchenAid

DESIGNER

Salvatore Manzo
Renaissance
663 Skippack Pike
Blue Bell, PA 19422
215.542.5000
www.renaissancekitchen.com

PHOTOGRAPHER: STEVE WHITSITT

This culinary
workspace was
transformed
from two
separate rooms.

culinary
splendor

Although new cabinets and appliances had been installed in this kitchen in order to sell this house, the new homeowners desired a remodel that would result in a more functional space, state-of-the-art appliances, better lighting and the incorporation of the adjacent Florida Room into an inviting eating space.

The original galley-style floor plan lacked ample counter space, and an existing deep and narrow built-in pantry created difficult access. Additional difficulties were caused by the location of the sink, which was placed on the end of one side of the galley.

Kitchen Designer, Janis Magnuson, CKD, of Kitchen Classics by Custom Crafters took the dysfunctional space to task by moving the sink to a corner location. This opened up counter space on each side while maintaining a view to the outside. The pantry was eliminated with the exception of a 15"-deep section, and it now serves as a nook for cookbooks and small appliances. Magnuson also constructed

bench seating and added it to the Florida Room to create additional eating space.

To complete the transformation, the kitchen entrance was enlarged with an arched opening; cherry wood cabinetry, stainless steel appliances, ceramic tile flooring, granite countertops and a slate backsplash were also incorporated into the design. Originally two separate rooms, this kitchen space now flows from a functional culinary workspace into a sun-streamed Florida Room overlooking the outside garden patio.◆

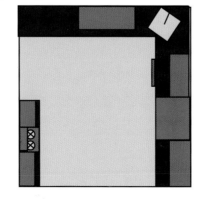

Special Features:
Adjacent Florida room with matching cabinetry; specialized lighting; enlarged arched opening to match living room arch; lighted nook

Dimensions:
Kitchen 11' x 13'
Florida room 9' x 12'

Products Used:
Cabinetry: Merit Kitchens, Whistler Door style; Cherry wood; Fired Earth finish
Flooring: Laufen ceramic tile
Countertops: Absolute Black granite
Sink: Elkay; 18-gauge stainless steel
Faucet: Grohe
Dishwasher: KitchenAid
Range: KitchenAid
Lighting: Tresco Xenon; Task Lumere
Refrigerator: KitchenAid
Wallcovering: Tile, California Gold slate in natural cleft
Microwave: GE
Disposal: KitchenAid
Hood: Sirius

DESIGNER

Janis M. Magnuson, CKD
Kitchen Classics by
Custom Crafters, Inc.
6023 Wilson Boulevard
Arlington, VA 22205
703.532.7000 x108

4000 Howard Ave.
Kensington, MD 20895
301.493.4000

PHOTOGRAPHER: BILL BUSCH

Light earth tones and black accents give the space dramatic contrast.

classic
kitchen

The client's existing kitchen was small and cramped. Even before approaching Fara Boico of Classic Kitchens they knew that they were going to extend the house and add more living space in order to increase the size of the kitchen. The client, who is an avid cook and enjoys entertaining, called upon Boico to create the space of their dreams.

The design challenge was to create a light, contemporary social environment that would allow the homeowner to work in the kitchen, while entertaining for guests and family. By placing the cooktop area across from the main sink, preparing food became more convenient. The cook could spread out while using the cooking surface and could just turn around, in her own domain to get to the sink. In the island by the main sink there was a lift up mixing center hidden away in a cabinet for food preparation. Guests could congregate both at the island and at the new expansive dinette area while enjoying a glass of wine from the wine refrigerator, while the cook is preparing food.

The color palate chosen for this contemporary kitchen were light earth tones combined with black accents to give the space a dramatic contrast of color. The russet apple cabinets, brown tan granite counter backsplash and mildly shaded porcelain tile floor all blended together in perfect harmony. Shapes of angled cabinetry added architectural accents and became a general theme throughout this kitchen design. The multi-level angled island was created to become the center and focal point of the kitchen.

Overall, the new space truly lives up to a timeless contemporary "Classic Kitchen." ◆

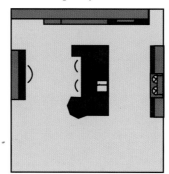

Special Features:
Multi-level counter on island; Lift-up mixing center in island cabinet; Contemporary octa-angle cabinets, wine refrigerator, desk area

Dimensions:
17' x 24'

Products Used:
Cabinetry: Neff
Flooring: Porcelain Tile
Countertops: Granite, brown tan
Sink(s): Franke
Faucets: Franke
Dishwasher: Asko
Cooktop: Wolf
Refrigerator: Sub-Zero
Wallcovering: Paint, faux finish
Oven: Wolf

DESIGNER

Fara Boico
Classic Kitchen & Bath
Center, Ltd.
1062 Northern Blvd.
Roslyn, NY 11576
516.621.7700

60B Jobs Lane
Southampton, NY 11968
631.204.9500

A curved, copper-clad island base was custom-made to mirror the copper detailing on the dramatic hood.

transformation
turns up aces

Sometimes the most wonderful projects can begin in the most innocent of ways.

The homeowner of this residence, set amid the rolling fairways and elegant lines of an award-winning golf course, started with a desire to just "patch the floor and possibly put in a new counter." The residence itself lived up to the promise of its setting, with a dramatic entry graced by the homeowner's impressive baby grand piano; however, the original kitchen showed little of the beauty surrounding it. Clearly, it needed more than a patch on the floor.

The homeowner hired David Frym and Ken D'Andrea of Northbay Kitchen & Bath to create a wonderful, calm oasis. One of the main objectives was to create a space where entertainment and sharing meals with friends was easy and interactive.

With entertainment in mind, the focal point of the room became the island and the attached granite eating area. A curved, copper-clad island base was custom-made

to mirror the copper detailing on the dramatic hood.

The height of the ceilings and the addition of recessed lighting all accentuated the drama of the finished project while the pale green ceramic tile and matching bookshelves brought the entire area together. The finishing touch was the perfect color match of the custom multi-finish stain of the cabinets to the Verde Gauguin counters and accent trim in the backsplash.

When the last detail was complete, this project was a perfect "hole in one."◆

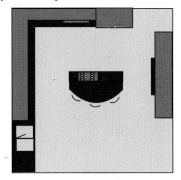

Special Features:
Full height Jeffery Court Chapter One backsplash. Cabinetry has distressed finish on raised doorstyle with contrasting rustic suede maple beadbacked interiors, apron front sink, custom copper and stainless steel hood, and low voltage lighting throughout

Dimensions:
17.5' x 15'

Products Used:
Cabinetry: Wood Harbor cabinetry
Flooring: Ceramic tile
Countertops: Verde Gauguin Slab Granite
Sink: Shaw Fluted Fireclay
Faucets: Rohl Country Class in oil-rubbed bronze
Dishwasher: KitchenAid
Cooktop: 36" Dynasty
Lighting: Recessed Ambiance under cabinet
Refrigerator: 36" KitchenAid
Wall Covering: Benjamin Moore warm tones
Oven: KitchenAid

DESIGNER

David Frym
Northbay Kitchen & Bath
822 Petaluma Blvd.
North
Petaluma, CA 94952
707.769.1646

DESIGNER

Salvatore Manzo
Renaissance
663 Skippack Pike
Blue Bell, PA 19422
215.542.5000

Photographer: John Martinelli

Decorative glass drawer fronts on the center island allow the homeowners to create their own elements of design.

a classic
country alcove

Special Features:
Bins, decorative hood, built-in hutch, antique glazed finish on cabinetry, rustic knobs

Dimensions:
32' x 17'6"

Products Used:
Cabinetry: Elmwood
Flooring: Oak Hardwood
Countertops: Granite
Sink(s): Franke
Faucets: Aquadis
Dishwasher: KitchenAid
Stove: Gallery Series Frigidaire
Refrigerator: KitchenAid

The homeowners chose to create a rendition of a country-style kitchen using originality and uniqueness. They wanted it to suit their two young children, but also be fit for entertaining family and friends. The homeowners hired Salvatore Manzo of Renaissance to capture the essence of this ideal kitchen.

A peninsula island between the sunroom and the kitchen creates a place to enjoy activities and snacks. This leaves the center island free for food preparation and entertaining guests. Tumbled marble on the backsplash creates texture against the silky hand-glazed cabinetry, which coordinates the soft mustard-colored granite on the countertops and islands.

A beautiful built-in hutch with a bead board interior allows for great storage, but also creates a charming focal point from the family room. A rustic wood top is added to the hutch to compliment the kitchen and the beautiful hardwood floors. Wicker baskets, placed in the center

island, add a country setting to the kitchen, but can also be used for storing fruit or useful household accessories.

By placing decorative glass drawer fronts on the center island, Manzo allows the homeowners to create their own elements of design. The mood of the kitchen changes throughout each season with items such as dried orange peels, peppermint leaves or potpourri. Creating elements such as these, Renaissance has ensured that this family will spend a lot of time in their wonderfully established kitchen.◆

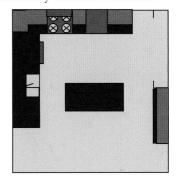

A French Country look is created through the careful blend of specialty moldings and washed cabinetry.

"lived-in" look

A challenge when designing a kitchen, in any new home, is how to keep the kitchen from looking too "new". This new space typically must blend with furniture the homeowners have acquired over the years. The owners of this newly built home requested a kitchen with a warm, French Country feel. Because they were planning to live in the home for many years to come, they wanted an environment with a timeless quality.

Gary A. Lichlyter, principal designer for Lemont Kitchen & Bath, Inc., achieved the homeowners' desires by suggesting cabinetry with a "washed" appearance paired with such details as specialty moldings and hardware that reflect a French Country history. At the homeowners' request, the island was designed using a contrasting stain than was used on the remainder of the kitchen. This gives the suggestion of an individual piece of furniture, as well as bringing additional visual interest to the room.

Another major request the homeowners' had was ample countertop space, something they did not have the luxury of in their previous kitchen. An island uninterrupted by a secondary sink or cooktop provides a generous amount of countertop space for meal planning and preparation.

Conveniences such as a commercial cooktop that makes meal preparation a snap, and a wine cooler and island baskets for specialty storage, blend beautifully in this "new" version of country living. ◆

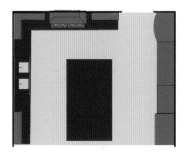

Special Features
Custom cooktop hood. Custom stained island with furniture legs. Specialty hardware and molding. Wine cooler.

Dimensions
13 feet by 16 feet

Products Used
Cabinetry: Custom by Lemont Kitchen and Bath, Acappella Island; Flooring: Hardwood; Countertops: Corian: Cameo White, island: Granite: Baltic Brown; Sink: Corian; Dishwasher: Bosch; Cooktop: Thermador; Refrigerator: SubZero; Oven: KitchenAid; Other: Microwave - KitchenAid, Wine Cooler - GE.

DESIGNER

Gary Lichlyter,
President and owner of
Lemont Kitchen and
Bath, Inc., has twenty
years of experience in
the kitchen and bath
industry. Contact the
designer at Lemont
Kitchen and Bath, Inc.,
106 Stephen St.,
Lemont, IL 60439,
630/257-8144.

PHOTOGRAPHER: STEVE WHITSITT

Warm wood tones and forest green distressed Bertch cabinetry create a striking juxtaposition against the warm tones.

elements
of nature

Nestled into the scenic hills of upstate New York, this new home called for a kitchen appropriate for entertaining business associates while comfortably accommodating a large, expanding family. Additional requirements included the need for the space to blend seamlessly into the rest of the home's décor, especially the adjacent great room.

The homeowners chose to work with Jenifer S. Young of Artisan Kitchens and Baths after discovering she had the ability to transform their desires into a space that would accomplish each of their objectives and complete their vision. The biggest design challenge was to create a separate space while drawing the kitchen into the adjacent great room. To meet this challenge, a virtual glass wall was created to divide the two rooms. Upper cabinets were designed with glass walls, doors and shelves to allow light to pass through. The base and trim were constructed of wood to ground it into the room.

The materials and finishes for the kitchen were chosen based on their ability to blend with elements of nature. Warm wood tones and forest green distressed Bertch cabinetry create a striking juxtaposition against the warm tones. Cabinets accented with glass doors add an element of reflected light. A dual-level island with warming drawer, wine captain, additional sink and dishwasher provide the homeowners with a multi-functional workspace by allowing food preparation to coincide with entertaining.◆

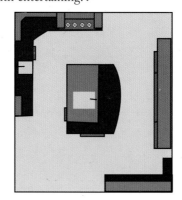

Special Features:
Dual-level island; wine captain; beverage center; custom pass through; stacked cabinets; dual dishwashers; apron-front stainless steel sink; custom stainless steel countertop

Dimensions:
26' x 19'

Products Used:
Cabinetry: Bertch
Countertops: Granite by Buffalo Granite & Marble, Stainless by ESKAY Metal Fabricating
Sink(s): Franke
Dishwasher: Bosch
Range: Wolf
Hood-Ventilation: Wolf
Refrigerator: Northland
Oven: Monogram
Flooring: Tile by The Tile Shoppe
Wine Captain: U-Line
Beverage Center: Monogram
Microwave: Monogram

PHOTOGRAPHER: STEVE PAUL WHITSITT

A working
triangle
and mini
vignettes were
incorporated
into the existing
layout to
increase
efficiency.

room with a
view

When deciding to renovate their home, these homeowners discovered their intra-coastal hideaway turned full-time residence was in need of more than a minor nip and tuck. The task at hand would be a major face lift, and transforming this outdated condo into a home worthy of its prestigious address involved a complete make over.

After taking note of the owners' lifestyle and their desires for the space, the primary goals became to create an open floor plan with a warm color palette and varying textures, and to transform the breakfast dining area into a space with a spectacular view of the neighboring waterway.

This dream space was accomplished with careful planning and great attention to detail. Walls were torn down to create a previously absent cohesion between the kitchen, living and formal dining rooms. Depth and warmth were created by using

glazed cherry thermo foil doors for the kitchen cabinets as well as the adjacent bar area. A working triangle and mini vignettes were incorporated into the existing layout to increase efficiency. The two-tiered peninsula provides grand counter space for occasional baking and a daily cup of coffee while enjoying the view. All said and done, this kitchen ended up being a joyous transformation and a "make over well done." ◆

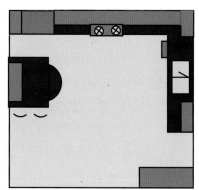

Special Features:
Multi-level peninsula; ModernAire copper hood; tumbled marble backsplash with granite tops; porcelain tile floor

Dimensions:
15' x 23'

Products Used:
Cabinetry: Ultracraft, Thermofoil
Sink(s): Kindred
Dishwasher: KitchenAid
Cooktop: Dacor
Refrigerator: KitchenAid
Wallcovering: Benjamin Moore paint
Hood: ModernAire
Hardware: Top Knobs

DESIGNER

Teri Turan
Blossom Brothers
Design Center
2706 N. Federal Hwy.
Delray Beach, FL 33483
561.274.7020

PHOTOGRAPHER: ROBERT LANGHAM

A farmhouse table and warm natural knotty alder create a country ambiance.

country
nostalgia

When these homeowners approached Samantha Fisher of Fisher Cabinet Works to design the kitchen for their new Lake Tyler, Texas home, they expressed their desire for the design to reflect a country farmhouse with a warm, nostalgic atmosphere. The couple also wanted to incorporate state-of-the-art appliances into the kitchen/butler's pantry without distracting from the country charm. Additionally, their wish list included an island to house the apron sink, dishwasher and compactor, while providing seating for family and friends and serving as a prep area.

Samantha worked to bring to life the homeowners' wishes by accommodating their requirements and providing them with a farm house table containing storage compartments accessible by concealed doors. Samantha also incorporated a beverage center, wine storage and an additional food prep area in the butler's pantry. The hammered copper sink, lowered mixing center and pull-down flour/sugar bins

reinforced the farm house design without sacrificing function.

Additional space was created by utilizing pull-out pantry systems, drawers for pots and pans, pull trays, a mixer lift, baking center and pull-out spice units. Other unique features include a farmer's grain bin, country hutch, buffet and custom appliance panels. Warm natural knotty alder is enhanced by splashes of red accents, flagstone cooktop surround, granite countertops, tumbled stone backsplash and tin ceiling.◆

Special Features:
Large, custom multi-level kitchen island; custom appliance panels on refrigerator and freezer; custom hutch, buffet

Dimensions:
17' x 8'

Products Used:
Cabinetry: Fisher Cabinet Works, Inc.
Countertops: Yellow Verona granite
Sink(s): American Standard
Dishwasher: Asko
Refrigerator/Freezer: Sub-Zero
Range: Wolf
Warming Drawer: Wolf
Compactor: KitchenAid

DESIGNER

Samantha Fisher
Fisher Cabinet
Works, Inc.
4556 FM 2813
Tyler, TX 75762
903.839.7129

PHOTOGRAPHER: STEVEN PAUL WHITSITT

A two-tiered island with built-in icemaker, microwave and secondary sink work in seamless harmony with the rest of the room.

the
entertainer

This Illinois kitchen perfectly matches its owners' desire to live large. As frequent entertainers, this family of four wanted a roomy kitchen with pizzazz. Designer Carol Begalka of Kitchen Gallery of Spring Grove was happy to oblige the clients—melding their wants and needs with a designer's vision. The result is a stunning room with function and beauty.

Begalka integrated custom cabinets with a unique combination of butternut-stained maple and smoky cherry to serve as the room's focal point. The multiple trim layers, which crest above the range hood, coax the eye upwards.

A two-tiered island with built-in ice-maker, microwave and secondary sink work in seamless harmony with the rest of the room. A peninsula supported at its tip by a pedestal contributes to the kitchen's open feel. It is just one of the many special touches in this new house, brought

to life by Begalka and Breckenridge Homes Inc. of McHenry. This creative collaboration resulted in a contemporary kitchen with amenities ranging from a double oven with warming drawer to a cookbook rack conveniently attached to a galley rail. Additional features include two double wastebasket cabinets to ease recycling, extra deep drawers and a pot filler mounted above the cooktop.◆

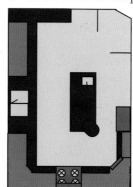

Special Features:
Raised microwave cabinet in island; maple cabinets with cherry doors; two-tone trim; peninsula supported by pedestal

Dimensions:
16' x 34'

Products Used:
Cabinetry: DuraSupreme
Flooring: Maple with inlay
Countertops: Zodiak
Dishwasher: Fisher Paykel
Cooktop: Thermador
Lighting: Can lights with pendants over peninsula
Refrigerator: Sub-Zero
Wallcovering: Paint
Oven: Wolf
Microwave: Dacor
Hood: Vent-A-Hood
Warming Drawer: Wolf

DESIGNER

Carol Begalka
Kitchen Gallery
of Spring Grove
2404 Spring Ridge Dr.,
Suite C
Spring Grove, IL 60081
815.675.6900

PHOTOGRAPHER: DANIEL FELDKAMP (VISUAL EDGE IMAGING)

Black Impala granite, antique distressed cabinets and new appliances give a new twist to this 1816's home.

colonial
appeal

This old country house was built in 1816, and it possessed a Colonial style the homeowners loved. The kitchen, however, was the one room that was devoid of the appeal of the rest of the house. Designer Kelly Zamonski was commissioned to create a kitchen that was modern and functional while tastefully embracing the home's colonial country charm.

Major priorities involved in the design of this kitchen included keeping ample storage and counter space without the use of an L-shaped countertop, which created a too-modern feel. In order to accomplish this, Zamonski decided to drop the right leg of the L-shape down to make it lower than standard countertops and to cut the depth to 14". She then suggested a wooden top to give it that old-world feel. Black Impala granite was used throughout the rest of the kitchen counters, and the homeowners utilized a solid piece of

walnut as the top for the lower section.

To continue the look, Zamonski installed antique distressed cabinets with beaded inset doors, split post columns on the island, and a china hutch with mullions and antique glass doors. The final touch was found in the wide planks and iron pegs the homeowners salvaged to use as flooring. ◆

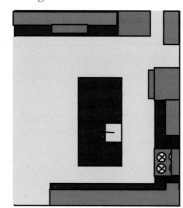

Special Features:
Salvaged old wood flooring; matching batten board inside display cabinets; fully integrated dishwasher in island

Dimensions:
16' x 16'

Products Used:
Cabinetry: Plain & Fancy Custom Cabinetry
Tile: IMG
Sink(s): Herbeau Creations of America
Faucets: Whitehaus
Dishwasher: KitchenAid
Range: Viking
Refrigerator: Sub-Zero
Oven: Viking
Warming Drawer: Viking

DESIGNER

Kelly Zamonski
The Kitchen Place, Inc.
1163 West Second St.
Xenia, OH 45385
937.372.6959

PHOTOGRAPHER: STEVE WHITSITT

Mission-style cabinetry with a natural Maple finish and hardwood flooring created warmth in the design.

challenging
spaces

This original kitchen was an outdated space with dysfunctional appliances and insufficient countertops. In order to make over the room, these Virginia homeowners were intricately involved in the decision-making process with designer Evelyn Nicely, president, Nicely Done Kitchens. Their collaborative efforts ensured the success of a clean, simple, unique design.

To substantially enlarge the existing sink area, Nicely relocated the refrigerator to another wall; this created ample counter space on either side of the sink. Additionally, a peninsula was added with a large arched countertop, and the double oven was replaced with a large 36" wide dual-fuel range and a more efficient microwave. An entertainment area was designed to allow viewing from the dining area, and the desk area was created with enough space for mailing, filing, storage and more. Mission-style cabinetry with a natural Maple finish and hardwood flooring created warmth in the design.

Among the notable design features of this space is a dual food preparation area. This area encourages unity for the family of four while cooking. Triangulated with this space are the desk/computer hutch and a home entertainment area. The creation of these spaces works to complement all areas of the room's functionality.◆

Special Features:
Customized entertainment center; workstation; 3-suite setting

Dimensions:
17' x 24'

Products Used:
Cabinetry: Holiday
Flooring: Hardwood
Countertops: Silestone, Blue Sahara
Sink(s): Oliveri
Faucets: Grohe
Dishwasher: Integrated
Range: Dacor 36"
Refrigerator: KitchenAid Overlaid

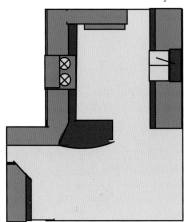

DESIGNER

Designer:
Evelyn Nicely
Nicely Done Kitchens
8934 Burke Lake Road
Burke, VA 22151
703.764.3748

PHOTOGRAPHER: DAVID VAN SCOTT

A European natural maple high gloss cabinet creates a modern effect.

dreams
realized

Dictated by a boomerang shape and barrel vault ceiling, this kitchen's defined cabinetry and eating area provided a design challenge. The space needed to involve visual movement without fighting the strong architectural elements of the space and not forgoing function.

Designer Alex Hall solved the dilemma by splitting the island into two separate entities. A larger island mimics the oblong shape of the walls and the cooktop area while providing additional seating. The smaller island has tubular chrome legs, a butcher block countertop, a six-inch stainless steel band that wraps around all four sides, and a built-in towel rack.

A European natural maple high gloss cabinet was chosen to create a modern effect; stainless steel was also incorporated into the cabinetry design. Stainless steel appliances reinforce the modern theme, and the contemporary design of the hood

makes it a focal point in the room. The warming drawer and dishwasher on the larger island are fully integrated and blend seamlessly into the symmetrical cabinet lines. Tall cabinets provide ample storage for the family's extensive china collection. A semi-tall glass cabinet with a flat, LCD television allows for convenient viewing from the snack counter or table.◆

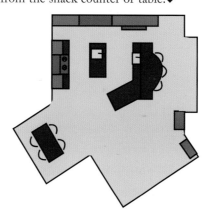

Special Features:
Barrel vault ceiling; two islands; European natural maple high gloss cabinets

Dimensions:
29' x 31'

Products Used:
Cabinetry: SieMatic
Flooring: Hardwood
Countertops: Granite; Butcher Block
Sink(s): Elkay
Faucets: Grohe
Dishwasher: Miele
Cooktop: Thermador
Refrigerator: Sub-Zero
Oven: Thermador
Microwave: GE
Warming Drawer: Dacor
Hood: Zephyr

DESIGNER

Alex R. Hall, CKD
The Creative Nook, Inc.
203 E. King Street
Malvern, PA 19355
610.644.6665

PHOTOGRAPHER: JEFF SCROGGINS

The island is composed of maple Shaker style cabinets featuring custom green paint with brown glaze.

endless
possibilities

This charming Rocky Mountain kitchen is a soothing space in the middle of an otherwise fast-paced household environment. The strong architectural presence of the red oak timber structural frame created a challenge for Linda Miller of Aspen Grove Kitchen and Bath Inc. Miller, who is both the designer and the homeowner, successfully overcame these challenges to create a beautiful, functional Colorado kitchen.

The cabinet layout was designed to fit within large posts, beams and knee braces. The island is composed of maple Shaker style cabinets featuring custom green paint with brown glaze, and the perimeter cabinets are natural cherry accented with glass doors. Details such as the simple columns on either side of the sink base provide attractive accents, while the columns by the range function as slide-out spice racks. Additional hidden accessories, such as pull-out wastebaskets, Lazy Susans, roll-out trays and slide-out towel bars create added functionality.

The resulting design has been successfully tested by family and friends who visit often to take advantage of the scenic Colorado landscape. Guests will frequently plan and prepare elaborate meals just to sample the kitchen's tools and appliances. Whether one cook or several, this space affords room for all to work comfortably.◆

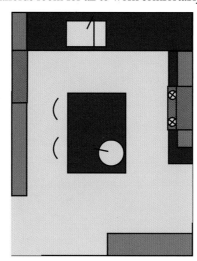

Special Features:
Custom sage green paint with brown glaze on island; pull-out spice rack columns on either side of range

Dimensions:
16' x 24'

Products Used:
Cabinetry: Brookhaven cherry/natural perimeter; Wood-Mode island
Flooring: TimberGrass Bamboo
Countertops: Giallo Juperano slab granite
Sink(s): Kohler under-mount
Faucets: Grohe; Newport Brass
Dishwasher: Bosch
Range: Dynasty 48"
Lighting: Hubbardton Forge
Refrigerator: Sub-Zero
Timberframe: Red Oak By Texas Timberframe
Hood: Best by Broan

DESIGNER

Linda G. Miller
Aspen Grove Kitchen
& Bath, Inc.
975 N. Ten Mile Drive
#E1
P.O. Box 860
Frisco, CO 80443
970.468.5393

Photographer: John Martinelli

The combination of appliances performs well enough to suit any chef.

preserving
history

The owners of this beautiful 1890's colonial home wanted to remove the contemporary kitchen installed by the previous owners. In its place they asked Salvatore Manzo of Renaissance to create a kitchen reminiscent of the home's original style, which also included all the modern conveniences for everyday living.

A combination of antique white painted cabinetry and KitchenAid stainless steel appliances was chosen for a classic feel. A furniture-styled island was added for convenient food preparation and to have a quick meal. The space included a butler's pantry adjacent to the kitchen. For this area, Manzo designed a blend of the original restored wall cabinetry with a wainscot backsplash and a custom-built base cabinetry finished by hand. This creation allowed for the additional room needed for granite counter surfaces, an extra sink and a second dishwasher.

The kitchen really cooks with a Thermador professional range, matching hood and a shelved backsplash. A built-in microwave tucked into the island, a 42-inch built-in refrigerator, fully integrated dishwasher, and a built-in stainless steel trash compactor all add to the polished look of the professional kitchen. Classic features include a handmade white brick tile backsplash with beautiful rope moldings and chair rail, beaded inset detail on the cabinetry, a large pantry cabinet with eight roll trays, glass doored display cabinets, and a built-in hutch. Each element helps to recreate the 1890's feel.

This delicate combination of period styling and modern features has become the heart of this much-loved home.◆

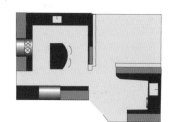

Special Features:
Large butler's pantry, brick tile backsplash, beaded inset cabinetry, glass door cabinetry, built-in hutch, 12" freeze board with multi level moldings, built in microwave in island.

Dimensions:
12'6" x 15'6"

Products Used:
Cabinetry: Renaissance Custom Cabinetry
Flooring: Oak Hardwood
Countertops: Granite
Sink(s): Kindred Collection
Faucets: Kohler
Dishwasher: KitchenAid
Stove: Thermador
Lighting: Tresco Under-Cabinet Lighting
Refrigerator: KitchenAid
Microwave: KitchenAid
Trash Compactor: KitchenAid
Knobs& handles: Top Knobs

DESIGNER

Salvatore Manzo
Renaissance
633 Skippack Pike
Blue Bell, PA 19422
215.542.5000

Photographer: Jim Stocker

The kitchen steps down into a connecting sunroom with a fireplace.

from contemporary stark
to old-world charm

The customer, an interior designer, came to fellow designer Dennis Regole, CKD, and his design coordinator, Rachelle Beardsley, of Charlestowne Kitchen & Bath with a project that challenged the imagination. The couple had purchased a resale house built in 1986 that offered great expanses of space but was lacking in style and warmth.

The design strategy was to transform this lifeless house into a charming old-world European home. The customer, by simple virtue of her background, was primarily interested in design and space usage. Every room needed to blend together with the next, yet at the same time have its own personality and key elements. All rooms were to provide a comfortable setting for entertaining family and friends.

The kitchen, with its 10-foot ceiling, was the primary task. The angled island, which echoes the unique floor plan, became the centerpiece. It incorporates a place to cook and provides seating for three, as well as storage. The eye is drawn across its surface to the large garden window behind the

sink. With a height of 103-inch from the floor the designers were allowed to utilize cabinetry and molding treatments to heights of 105-inch and more. The soffits are placed at various heights to conceal beams and plumbing while also providing a strong design statement.

The kitchen steps down into a connecting sunroom with a fireplace, which is visible from the kitchen. The fireplace was given a whole new old-world look. It completes the customer's wish for warmth and comfort. The entire design team transformed this house into a comfortable, inviting place for family and friends to gather. ◆

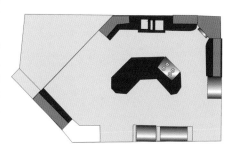

Special Features:
Special angled island to fit unique floor plan, large garden window, ten foot ceilings allowing cabinets and crown molding to be set at 105". Connecting sunroom with Fireplace remodeled to oldworld look; custom designed canopy wood hood over BarBQ grill; special valance.

Dimensions:
28' x 18.5'

Products Used:
Cabinetry: Crystal Cabinets
Flooring: Imported Italian marble
Countertops: Granite
Sink: Elkay,
Faucets: Kohler
Dishwasher: Bosch
Cooktop: Fisher & Paykel
Lighting: Halogen
Refrigerator: Sub-Zero
Wallcovering: Textured Wallpaper
Oven: KitchenAid
Trash Compactor: KitchenAid
Grill: Thermador Char-Glo
Microwave: GE

By placing the sink in the island, an efficient work triangle is formed.

country
warmth

Special Features:
Honed blue pearl granite, decorative ceiling design, furniture-style hutch, cherry cabinetry

Dimensions:
16.5' x 21'

Products Used:
Cabinetry: Jay Rambo Co.
Flooring: Limestone
Countertops: Honed Blue Pearl, Carrera Marble, Wood Desktop
Sink(s): Elkay Undermount
Faucet: Grohe Europlus II
Dishwasher: KitchenAid
Cooktop: Caldera
Lighting: Tresco International
Refrigerator: KitchenAid
Oven: KitchenAid
Warming Drawer: KitchenAid

When the homeowners took possession of this early 1930's home, they knew they would need to renovate the kitchen to accommodate their busy lifestyle. With an active family, including school-age children and a love for entertaining, the current space was not adequate. Their top priority for the new room, in addition to many kitchen accessories, was to combine a family area within the kitchen area. "And we wanted a large, open space with plenty of light," explained the homeowner.

The solution was a complete gut of the current kitchen space and the addition of a family room. The homeowners sought the advice of kitchen specialist Gary A. Lichlyter of Lemont Kitchen & Bath to help bring to fruition their vision for the new kitchen. Collaborating with the architect and interior designer, Lichlyter designed a kitchen that would complement the rest of the home while addressing the needs of a contemporary family.

With plenty of space, Lichlyter designed an island large enough to provide comfortable seating with plenty of countertop space for meal preparation and clean up. By placing the sink in the island, an efficient work triangle is formed. Traditional cherry cabinetry with subtle moldings were chosen and finished with crystal knobs. A message center keeps schedules in constant view. All-natural materials, including honed granite, marble and wood, were chosen for the countertops. Adding to the understated grace of the new kitchen is an X-patterned ceiling designed and executed by the architect.

Function and form blend beautifully in this newly designed kitchen and family area, which has truly become the heart of this home.◆

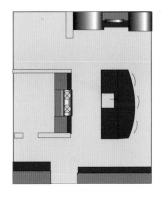

Photographer: Steve Whitsitt

The kitchen reflects the owner's love of the California gold country.

Special Features:
Verdi Mankia granite counters and full-height backsplash, glass front stacked cabinets with a distressed finish on raised door style. Old boot black and barn red finish with contrasting butternut maple bead-backed interiors, rustic hickory pecan floors and doors, apron front sink, custom etched glass accents and low voltage lighting throughout.

Dimensions:
22.5' x 15'

Products Used:
Cabinetry: Dura Supreme Designer Series
Flooring: Rustic Hickory Pecan
Countertops: Slab Granite
Sink: Rohl Apron Sink
Faucets: Rohl Country Collection
Dishwasher: KitchenAid
Range: KitchenAid
Lighting:Recessed
Refrigerator: KitchenAid
Wall covering: Kelly Moore Warm Tones
Oven: KitchenAid

california
dreaming

Every now and then a designer is given a plum assignment, a dream client and the request to "pull out all the stops." When that happens, work seems to end and creative playtime begins. When David Frym, owner of Northbay Kitchen & Bath, told Ken D'Andrea, his designer, that he was going forward in his kitchen remodel, it was a case of dusting off the plans that David had fine tuned for years and been talking about with Ken for almost as long.

"There were times in the process," said D'Andrea, "that it seemed like there was one mind putting this kitchen together." The level of detail in this project required a strong working relationship between the two professionals. The communication over the years and the many projects they had completed together clearly resulted in the highest levels of craftsmanship and design.

Frym had always wanted a home that projected his love of the California "gold country" and was a dramatic backdrop for his extensive collection of mining artifacts. This kitchen, with its many design features, certainly accomplished that goal. After all, it's not the everyday kitchen that has authentic ore carts gracing its perimeter.

With one part of the team working on the cabinet details, the other part of the team filled the role of interior designer. Frym exhibited the fine eye of a very talented interior designer pulling all of the elements together to complete this stunning residence. This project shows that this homeowner knows what "design/build" really means.◆

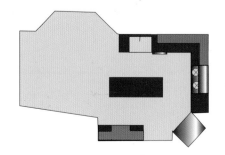

DESIGNER

David Frym & Ken D'Andrea
Northbay Kitchen & Bath
822 Petaluma Blvd. North
Petaluma, CA 94952
707.769.1646

Photographer: Peter Malinowski, In-Site Photography

The application detail of the cedar ceiling camouflages numerous roofhips and structural obstacles.

thinking outside
the box

This central coast California family had worked with their architect to plan an extensive remodel of their ranch home. They felt the kitchen should highlight their updated great room and were disappointed that concepts presented were so ordinary. Patricia Knight, ISID, met the couple through some satisfied clients, and she assured them that she could think "outside of the box."

The wife, an enthusiastic cook, was fanatical about storage and having plenty of floor space for guests and family to socialize without getting under foot. Her husband wanted a modern feel and specifically requested that the cabinets have legs. Because the family has two small dogs, a charismatic cat and a young daughter in the residence, Knight designed a recessed toe box that disappears into the ceramic tile floor while appearing to float on appliance legs.

Knight, known for her passion of efficient storage and use of distinctive materials, used the new custom front door (not in view) as the central theme for unusual color combinations. She recommended a Shaker cabinet door with exaggerated rails and stiles, in her favorite cherry wood, and lichen green finish to create a can-

vas for other materials. Working in collaboration with the clients, Knight designed and sourced the custom tongue and groove cedar ceiling. The application detail camouflages numerous roof hips and structural obstacles while showcasing the artistry of the finish carpenter and patience of the general contractor. The same custom mill was contracted for the 10-foot-long solid mahogany bar top. Knight then carried the material's elements of wood, slate and stainless steel into the design and styling of the fireplace.

Each of the major zones, from the L-shaped cooking and clean-up, communication center, work island and casual dining to the fireplace and entry, now repeat a variation of the original theme. Not only have the homeowners' expectations been fulfilled but far surpassed ◆

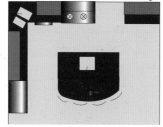

Special Features:
Communication center includes: stereo components; 18" opening at base for pet dishes and deep drawer for pet food; wine captain and cubbies for CDs and wine. Fluted glass detail is repeated on custom front door, pantry door and cabinets. Legs, in lieu of toe kick, makes the cabinets appear to float.

Dimensions:
11' x 20'

Products Used:
Cabinets: Merit
Flooring: Ceramic Tile
Counters: Labradour Antique
Wood Top: Custom Mahogany
Backsplash Tile: Slate
Sink(s): Kindred
Faucets: Grohe
Hardware: Top Knobs
Range: Dacor
Warming Drawers: Dacor
Ventilation: Best
Dishwasher: Fisher & Paykel
Microwave: Sharp
Refrigerator: Sub-Zero
Wine Captain: U-Line

DESIGNER

Patricia J.Knight
PJ Knight Kitchens, Inc.
2264 Lillie Avenue,
Suite 3
Summerland, CA 93067
805.565.0460

Photographer: David Van Scott

Varying countertop materials and using contrasting cabinet colors visually defines the space.

kitchen
discoveries

The first consultation with these clients included the review of a detailed wish list. After initial budgetary concerns and considerations, the project sat idle for many weeks. The clients weighed other options, such as moving, and then realized that buying a new home would still not give them the kitchen of their dreams. So when they decided to move forward with drawings of the addition and new kitchen, they contacted Alex R. Hall, CKD, of The Creative Nook, and the excitement began.

The initial challenge of the new space was the selection and use of windows to make an architectural statement. The additional expense of round-top windows was an easy decision once the three-dimensional computer drawings revealed their overall effect in the 12-foot addition with vaulted ceilings. These windows reveal a beautiful view of the sun setting over a local river.

Providing the clients with a kitchen for frequent entertaining was the next challenge. Hall solved this with a large, 10-foot, two-tiered island with seating for four. The island houses a double bowl sink, dishwasher, trash compactor, recycling container and a 30-inch warming drawer. The length of the island dictated its width and its position in the room. The extensive appliance package was completed on the exterior L-shape with the integrated Sub-Zero, double ovens and a 48-inch professional cook top. A prep sink was also added.

Varying countertop materials and using contrasting cabinet colors visually defines the space. The custom cabinets are full overlay, square raised panel with imported knobs and pulls. The main L-shape is maple with a coffee stain and glaze while the hutch and island are painted maple with brown glaze. The unique hutch displays a special collection of wine and champagne taken from the clients' existing wine cellar.

Other notable features are the custom stucco and wood hood, which incorporates the tumbled marble used for the backsplash, the recessed niche over the cook top and the Australian cypress floor installed in random widths, which was carried into the adjoining dining room.◆

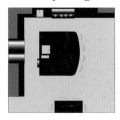

Special Features:
Two, 4-foot twin casement palladium windows alongside the custom stucco and wood hood. The hood is the focal point in the new vaulted ceiling addition.

Dimensions:
21' x 25'7"

Products Used:
Cabinetry: Lewistown
Flooring: Australian Cypress
Countertops: Granite and butcher block
Sink(s): Elkay
Faucets: Grohe
Dishwasher: KitchenAid
Cooktop: DCS
Lighting: Hera Under-cabinet and Juno Recessed
Refrigerator: Sub-Zero
Oven: KitchenAid
Trash Compactor: KitchenAid
Warming Drawer: KitchenAid
Microwave: KitchenAid

DESIGNER

Alex R. Hall, CKD
The Creative Nook, Inc.
203 E. King Street
Malvern, PA 19355
610.644.6665

Photographer: Steve Whitsitt

An antique stained-glass dome is placed in the ceiling.

a victorian
mansion

Tradition and technology happily coexist in this complete renovation of a Victorian home. Preserving the structure's historical character without sacrificing modern convenience was the challenge for designer Chris Dreith, of The Home Improvements Group.

To retain the home's historic charm, Dreith incorporated a number of features commonly found in 19th-century kitchens and gave them a modernist twist. She created a focal point by placing a 10-foot antique stained-glass dome in the ceiling. The inverted bowl reigns over the dual islands adorned with granite countertops and a period sink. The islands, anchoring the kitchen's expanse of oak and mahogany floor, create additional room for meal preparation. An adjoining maple shelf provides a serving area adjacent to a pair of stunning French doors replete with leaded and beveled glass.

Period workstation furniture from YesterTec accommodates and conceals high-tech appliances. The rich character of cherry and mahogany complements the home's historic features. Ambient lighting across the tops of the tall furniture provides a staging area for a collection of heirlooms and art pieces.

Appliances were selected to facilitate meal preparation and food and utensil storage. A state-of-the-art oven and microwave are hidden behind unobtrusive pocket doors that slide into the patented UL approved workstation, simultaneously triggering an internal electrical system to activate the ovens.

Custom-designed punched-tin panels embellish the central piece's pocket doors, providing winsome historic flair.◆

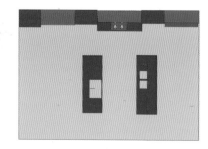

Special Features:
Furniture cabinets that hide appliances, two islands, antique stained glass ceiling, designed for one cook or many caterers, custom design on punched tin panels.

Dimensions:
15' X 25'

Products Used:
Cabinetry: Yestertec
Flooring: Hard wood
Countertops: Granite
Sink(s):Vermont soapstone, Elkay
Faucets: Whitehaus
Dishwasher: Bosch
Cooktop: GE
Refrigerator: Sub-Zero
Oven:GE
Other: Knobs: Top Knobs; Country Accents punched tin
Wallcovering: Bradberry & Bradberry wallpaper

DESIGNER

Chris Dreith
The Home
Improvements Group
Inc.
440 Main Street
Woodland, CA
95695
530.666.5061

DESIGNER

Chris Dreith
CKD, CBD
The Home
Improvements Group
Inc.
440 Main Street
Woodland, CA
95695
530.666.5061

Photographer: Steve Whitsitt

The kitchen showcases a collection of world pottery.

sun-splashed
tuscan

Special Features:

Unique shaped island with banquet seating, bronze colored glass tiles set in tumbled marble backsplash, stainless steel range set at angle, skylight shaft lighted with hidden fixtures.

Dimensions:
18' X 24'

Products Used:

Cabinetry: Merit
Flooring: Satillo tile
Countertops: Giallo
Sinks: Rohl
Faucets: Whitehaus, Chicago faucets
Dishwasher: Bosch
Cooktop: Dacor
Lighting: Seagull, Task, Tresco
Refrigerator: Sub-Zero, U-line
Knobs: Top Knobs, Cliffside
Warming oven : Dacor
Microwave: Dacor

A sun-splashed taste of Tuscany welcomes guests to this light and warm kitchen in a completely remodeled home. The owners wanted a space that was fun to cook in and that would double as a showcase for their extensive collection of brightly colored pottery.

Designer Chris Dreith, of The Home Improvements Group, created a spacious setting by absorbing 8 feet of garage space. In the process, she pulled the kitchen area out of the home's busy traffic corridor and made an airy opening into the newly expanded family room.

This extra space allowed room for a uniquely shaped island to provide a centerpiece for the area. Set above a floor of bright Saltillo tile, the island's tiered granite countertops are infused with a range of golds, browns and pomegranate-hued bits of garnet. Tumbled marble backsplashes, seeded with bronze glass, complement the countertops. A banquet-style seat, ensconced in the V-shaped configuration of the island,

overlooks the family room, providing a casual perch that invites visitors to kibitz with the cook.

A cozy window seat, roomy desk and expansive bar—with its own undercounter refrigerator, sink and storage space—occupy the renovated kitchen area. A series of lively nooks, niches and shelves run throughout, housing the engaging display of world pottery.

Recessed ceiling lights emblazon a new skylight. Three forged-iron pendant lights bathe the island below in an amber glow. The earthy richness of the cabinet's maple with chocolate chalking provides a warm ambiance to this lively home.◆

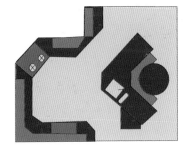

DESIGNER

Amee K. McNamara, CKD
Blackdog Builders Inc.
7 Red Roof Lane
Unit #1
Salem, NH 03079
603.898.0868

Photographer: Bill Fish

It took starting from scratch to create this kitchen wonder.

paying
homage

Special Features:
Butler's pantry, multi-level island, entertainment unit with large desk, custom cabinet to camouflage air conditioner, bas-relief tiles on backsplash

Dimensions:
24' x 27'- kitchen
7' x 7' - butler's pantry

Products Used:
Cabinetry: Plato, cherry
Countertops: Tropical Red and Green granite and Vanilla Rose marble
Sink(s): Whitehaus, Kohler
Faucets: Whitehaus
Dishwasher: Fisher & Paykel
Cooktop: Jenn-Air
Refrigerator: Sub-Zero
Wallcovering: Benjamin Moore
Oven: Thermador
Wine Cooler: Marvel

From between fierce marble lions, a driveway sweeps toward a stately Victorian home. No gingerbread or Easter basket colors here—this home is a venerable structure of thickly rounded turrets and a sensible shade of green, a respected dowager on a street of historic homes.

In older homes, bad remodeling and haphazard fix-ups accumulate over time. The kitchen had mutated into a narrow gallery that stretched from what was formerly the butler's pantry. An oversized hood dwarfed a long, anorexic island. Previous homeowners had attempted to create a cozy den by walling off one quarter of the room and finishing it with round-cornered, heavily textured plastering reminiscent of an adobe hut. Amee K. McNamara, CKD, knew that a full gut was in order.

The butler's pantry was reclaimed while the bulk of the kitchen was brought forward, and now a two-tiered island allows

the cook to preside over gatherings. The den was removed, but McNamara retained function and coziness by incorporating a seating area, defined by an entertainment center and a desk. Arch-top windows show off the landscaping and pool, creating a backdrop for the dramatic 60-inch diameter table. A custom cabinet hides the air conditioner, while a hutch with furniture details and marble top provides storage. A new tin ceiling restores the elegance of decades past.

The old house, having been paid her proper due, seems satisfied.◆

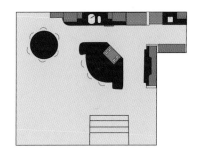

DESIGNER

Guita Behbin
Dura Maid Industries, Inc.
130 Madison Avenue
New York City, NY 10016
212.686.0246

Photographer: Peter Ledwith

The new counter creates the illusion of a "U" shaped kitchen.

warm &
contemporary

Special Features:
Cabinets made of two wood species and in two finishes. Hardwareless doors and drawers. Stainless steel backsplash, multilevel upper cabinets and eating counter

Dimensions:
12'6" x 9'

Products Used:
Cabinetry: Brookhaven
Flooring: Limestone
Countertops: Granite
Sink: Franke
Faucets: Franke
Dishwasher: Bosch
Cooktop: Dacor
Lighting: Halogen
Refrigerator: Sub-Zero
Wallcovering: Paint
Oven: Dacor

On the upper west side of Manhattan is a fabulous pre-war apartment with classic woodworking details and very high ceilings. The kitchen previously was very poorly laid out and in stark contrast to the rest of the home, was plain in style and basic in material. So the room was gutted and redesigned to fit the needs of the owners who are a very busy couple with their own business and a young daughter with lots of extracurricular activities like ballet. Their busy life caused them to want a simple, comfortable and functional kitchen with a well-lit, bright feel and user-friendly accessories. So the kitchen is remodeled and given a contemporary design, intentionally keeping in stark contrast with the home.

After the removal of two walls and relocation of appliances, the designer, Guita Behbin of Dura Maid Industries, was able to give the clients all that they asked for and more. She concealed and integrated structural columns with a tall pantry on one corner and a spice cabinet and countertop on another, which resulted in a better flowing design and the maximum use of space.

The resulting extra width allows for an eating counter, which wraps around and connects each side of the room and provides enough space for two or three people. At the end of each cabinet run are towers that were created by extending the cabinets above the refrigerator and the tall pantry up to the ceiling. Molding detail crowns them and sets them apart from the rest of the kitchen, which is lower in height. This multilevel effect makes for visual interest and accentuates the high ceiling in an otherwise square space. The cabinets were made of two wood species with a gray stain on the oak for the cabinet frame and natural finish on maple for the doors and drawers. The granite countertops and limestone floor complement the colors of the cabinetry. The stainless steel backsplash also pulls together and communicates the underlying design concept of contemporary simplicity and pizzazz in this kitchen.◆

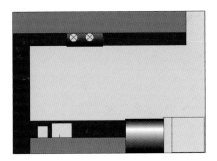

DESIGNER

Rochelle Kalisch, CKD,
Regency Kitchens, Inc.,
4204 14th Ave.,
Brooklyn, NY 11219
718.435.4266
Fax 718.435.5411

204 E. 77th Street, Ste. 1E
New York, NY 10021
212.517.8707

A bronze
decorative
hood
positioned on
the back-
ground of a
white Carrara
marble wall
provides the
focal point.

a millennium
showhouse

Special Features:
Custom-designed hood
and hardware, mosaic
backsplashes and floor.

Dimensions:
14' x 10'

Products Used:
Custom Cabinets:
Regency;
Cooktop, Undercounter
ovens and Dishwasher:
Gaggenau; Microwave:
GE; Refrigerator: Sub-
Zero 27"; Vent hood:
Best; Undercounter
wine cooler: Marvel
stainless steel;
Washer/dryer:
Whirlpool; Lighting:
Juno halogen;
Granite: International
Stone and Accessories

As 1999 drew to a close, 30 New York decorators and designers were invited to redecorate a turn-of-the-19th-century townhouse on Manhattan's Upper East Side. Proceeds of the venture went to major Manhattan charities.

The original space given to Certified Kitchen Designer Rochelle Kalisch of Regency Kitchens, Inc., was a main kitchen with dinette and laundry/storage room. The kitchen, built in the 1970s, had white Formica cabinets, black granite countertops and a granite checkerboard floor. The overall effect was gloomy and out of context with the architecture of the house. The layout was cramped and dark, and natural light was blocked by a cabinet and partitions.

To create a light, spacious and inviting kitchen, the designer created a U-shaped plan with a center island, open toward the dinette and removed partitions to unify the room. A butler's pantry and desk area was placed in the former laundry room.

Cabinetry was chosen to link the room to the house's history—old-fashioned beaded inset oak, painted in farmhouse red, with textured glass inserts. Elements of arts and crafts style also capture the flavor of the time in the hardware and bar stools, designed especially for this project.

In order to create a rich and dramatic interior, a wide variety of materials was used: Floors and backsplashes are terra cotta and white Carrara marble tiles; the same marble is used on countertops. A vivid yellow floral wallpaper warms the space, as do the aged copper faucets.

State-of-the-art appliances make the finished kitchen not only a design statement but a perfectly functioning food-processing laboratory for the 21st century. ◆

DESIGNER

Gayle E. Smith
Kitchen Gallery of Spring
Grove
2404 Spring Ridge Drive,
Suite C
Spring Grove, IL 60081
815.675.6900

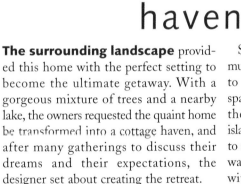

The owners requested the quaint home be transformed into a cottage haven.

Special Features:
Antique white w/rubbed off edges; Multi-level island to accommodate microwave; Glass doors to add decorative touch to the island.

Dimensions:
10'6" X 14'6"

Products Used:
Cabinetry: Bridgewood/Jim Bishop Cabinetry
Flooring: Oak
Countertops: Granite by Granite Edge
Sink(s): Blanco
Faucets: Grohe
Dishwasher: Bosch
Refrigerator: Sub-Zero
Range: Jenn-Air-Down Draft
Microwave: G.E.

a cottage
haven

The surrounding landscape provided this home with the perfect setting to become the ultimate getaway. With a gorgeous mixture of trees and a nearby lake, the owners requested the quaint home be transformed into a cottage haven, and after many gatherings to discuss their dreams and their expectations, the designer set about creating the retreat.

Inspired by the assortment of textures and colors on the outside of the home, designer Gayle Smith and the homeowners created a similar combination in the interior décor.

The house layout allotted very little space for the kitchen, so Smith was challenged to create storage in the room that would accommodate all of the owners' kitchen items. But she also allowed for personal and other decorative items to be integrated into the design scheme. The tall wall cabinet with glass doors serves well for a focal touch with lighting installed inside. The glass shelves add a touch of glimmer to the glass dishes, which are artfully presented.

Smith agreed with her clients that the multi-level island would be an efficient area to place the microwave and also a great space for entertaining as well. She placed the glass doors on the backside of the island to add drama to the open room. And to add a bit of contrast, a small cherry trim was added to the crown to help the flow with the antiqued white cabinets, wood floor and the natural stone.

The result was a kitchen that not only met the family's cooking and entertaining needs, but also reflected their personal style and tastes. ◆

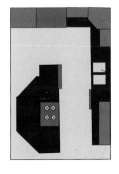

DESIGNER

Patricia Knight
Tim Bates, CKCD
P. J. Knight Kitchens, Inc.
1187 Coast Village Rd.
Suite 1 #526
Santa Barbara, CA   93108
805.565.0460

2264 Lille Ave., #3
Summerland, CA 93067
805.565.0460

Photographer: Peter Malinowski

This couple's collaboration has resulted in the fusion of storage, function, socializing and fashion.

Special Features:
Mini-storage left of refrigerator accommodates more than 100 items and nothing lost from view;
Cabinet detail and tile design create a strong hearth effect at the ventilation hood;
Foot pedal allows hands-free faucet operations.

Dimensions:
18.5' X 11'

Products Used:
GreenField Custom Select Cabinetry, Beaded Inset
Flooring: Turkish Travertine
Counters: Juparana Bordo Granite
Backsplash Tile: Tumbled Scabos & Ahnzu
Sinks & Faucet: Kindred & Grohe
Hardware: Top Knobs
Pedal Works: Pedal Value
Range: Dacor
Ventilation: Sirius
Dishwasher: Miele
Microwave: Quasar
Refrigerator: Amana

dueling
designers

With their own kitchen and bath design firm, this couple had separate approaches to design, and they wanted to incorporate all ideas in their Central Coast California town home. Both had firm opinions as to how to design their project, and after many design revisions and "discussions," they agreed upon a design.

The wife, an enthusiastic cook, was fanatical about storage and having a bar height area for guests and family to socialize without getting under foot. She also wanted styling options to showcase her artistic flair. The husband, a Connecticut transplant, is schooled in architecture and insisted upon proportion and balance while blending in traditional East Coast style.

The beaded inset cabinetry provides a fine furniture feel and the kitchen area is stained and glazed cherry wood. The hutch area, which incorporates bar height casual dining and a family communications center, is detailed with beaded paneling,

painted off-white and glazed. The Juparana Bordo granite counters complement the cabinetry and the splash's gloss field tile, arranged in a brick pattern that emulates the feel of a warm fireplace. Tumbled Scabos marble accent tiles create a subtle contrast in texture and size. Additional cabinets in the adjacent laundry room provide storage for infrequently used kitchen items. The custom designed mantel range hood conceals a powerful and quiet hood liner operated by remote control.

All agree that this couple's collaboration has resulted in the fusion of storage, function, socializing and fashion. The duel is a draw. ◆

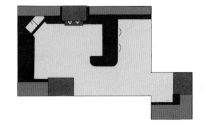

THE BEST OF SIGNATURE KITCHENS 225

DESIGNER

Carol Lindell
Design Centers
International, LLC
DCI Home Resource
1300 South Blvd., Suite C
Charlotte, NC 28203
704.926.6000

Photographer: Michael LoBlondo

The horseshoe-shaped dining bar has become the center for casual family conversation.

the hub of
activity

Special Features:
Double islands accommodate both a baking center and serving area, with double-stacked wall cabinetry proportional to 12-foot ceiling

Dimensions:
20' X 24'

Products Used:
Cabinetry: Quality Custom
Flooring: Stone
Countertops: Granite
Sink(s): Franke
Faucets: Franke
Dishwasher: Bosch
Range: Viking
Refrigerator: Sub-Zero
Wine and refrigerator drawers: Sub-Zero
Ice Maker: Scotsman

As the heart of an active family's elegant home, this outstanding kitchen created by Design Centers International of Charlotte is a true showstopper. Challenged to create both a functional and warm family kitchen that would accommodate multiple cooks, this floor plan includes various activity zones.

The cooking and food preparation area features a Viking range with pot-filler faucet by Franke and an island that includes easy-to-access Sub-Zero refrigerator drawers, an undercounter microwave oven and Franke prep sink. For ease in entertaining, Sub-Zero wine storage and an ice machine round out the center island area, with design accents featuring turned posts and furniture base trim.

The horseshoe-shaped dining bar has become the center for casual family conversation, in close proximity to the adjacent breakfast bar featuring the Sub-Zero refrigerator, family microwave and hidden pantries with touch-latch wainscot

panel access. Large double walk-in pantry doors match the stain and glazed maple cabinetry, with custom iron panels accenting each door. The nearby family desk and message center provides a focus point for notes, electronics, keys and family communications.

For quick clean up, double dishwashers flank the main sink, with each dishwasher hidden behind fully integrated cabinetry panels. Additional specialty cabinets are also featured, including appropriately placed trash pullouts, tray cabinets and dish drawers.

As the hub for this active family's home, this kitchen is a proven success—both in function and as the heart of a phenomenal residence. ◆

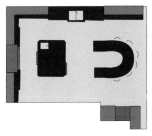

DESIGNER

Ellyn Gutridge
Custom Crafters, Inc.
4000 Howard Ave.
Kensington, MD 20895
Phone: 301.493.4000

The rich grain of cherry cabinets and stainless steel appliances make this kitchen shine.

Special Features:
21" Wood medallion in floor; stainless steel leg supports; eating peninsula; shift 1/2 bath out to hall access, creating a butler's area, which connects sitting room with kitchen.

Dimensions:
13.5' X 11.5'
plus 6 X 6 butler's area

Products Used:
Cabinetry: Kountry Kraft, Clearfield Cherry
Flooring: M & M Floors, Inc.
Countertops: Marblex, Sahara Beige Granite
Sink: Elkay #ELU2221 Lustertone
Faucets: Grohe #33759 Lady Lux Plus
Dishwasher: Bosch # SHU 6805
Range: Dacor # SGM 365
Refrigerator: KitchenAid # KSSC36QKS
Wine Captain: KitchenAid # KUWS 246E66
ISE Hotwater Dispenser
Hood: Sirius #SU201
Stainless steel leg

inviting comfort
from all angles

What could be more enjoyable than a glass of wine with the cook while dinner simmers? A seat by the fire, of course. Before Ellyn Gutridge of Custom Crafters Inc. worked her magic on this center hall Colonial in Chevy Chase, Md., the kitchen was cloistered in the back of the house. A den and full bath were isolated in the front. By downsizing to a smaller powder room with access from the hall and removing several walls, cozy and cooking could now communicate.

"The clients loved the design and had total faith in us while we worked out the construction details, but there were challenges," Gutridge said. An angled wall supporting the stairs affected what could be done with the half-bath plumbing and the placement of the KitchenAid refrigerator. "It became all about working with angles."

The resulting bridge that joined the rooms became the perfect spot for a wine captain and wine racks. Open display and glass-front cabinetry show off mementos above a buffet area that holds large serving pieces. A 21-inch medallion enlivens the wood floor as no rug could.

The kitchen shines with stainless steel appliances, hardware and a sleek hood. Contemporary pendant lights and a custom-made stainless steel support for the granite peninsula are warmed with the rich grain of cherry cabinets and a variegated, textured tile backsplash.

The sitting room boasts a gas fireplace and comfortable armchairs. Overall the effect is sophisticated, yet comfortable and inviting. ◆

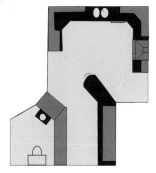

Photographer: David Kielpinski/Nippersink Studio

Maple cabinetry
and granite
countertops are
a striking
combination.

teamwork with
tantalizing results

Kitchen designer Tracey Paulson truly captured a couple's love of textures and simplicity. The result: a kitchen that is both beautiful and functional.

Working with both the homeowners and the builder, Jim Mihovilovich, Jr., they agreed on the mixture of the warm, natural look of maple cabinetry, the striking combination of the granite countertops, and the bold Baltic blue island to make this an aesthetically appealing kitchen with a sophisticated living space.

Lighting was also crucial in creating a successful space. Over-cabinet and under-cabinet lighting both contribute to the ambience in this kitchen. Recessed cans and dramatic pendant lighting create general illumination as well as drama to the island.

Paulson created the island to be a multitask area. Preparation space was important, as wall as a raised bar area that she provided for social gatherings or that morning cup of coffee.

To enhance the island, the designer added a glass cabinet on the end to provide a focal point, drawing you visually into the island space.

"This kitchen was a key element in this home," Paulson said, "and by working as a team, we provided the necessary detail to meet our clients' needs."◆

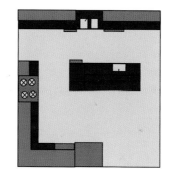

Special Features:
Multilevel island; maple floor with cherry inlay; stainless steel back-splash; complementary granite at island and perimeter.

Dimensions:
16' X 17'

Products Used:
Cabinetry: Merit Cabinetry (Frameless)
Flooring: Maple Wood Floor with Cherry inlay
Countertops: Sapphire Brown Granite at perimeter, Bianco lavender at island
Sinks: Oliveri stainless undermount for kitchen & island
Faucets: Grohe
Dishwasher: Bosch integral
Cooktop: Dacor Epkure 36" cooktop with Viking S.S. Hood
Lighting: Custom lighting
Refrigerator: Viking Bottom mount
Oven: Dacor 30" Double oven
Warming drawer: Dacor 30"
Trash compactor: KitchenAid

230   **THE BEST OF SIGNATURE KITCHENS**

DESIGNER

Tracey L. Paulson
Kitchen Gallery of
Spring Grove
2404 Spring Ridge
Dr.ive Suite C
Spring Grove, IL 60081
Phone: 815.675.6900

Photographer: Steve Weigert

The slightly
honed granite
counters mirror
the history of
the site.

bringing the great
outdoors in

Nestled in the rustic surroundings of a 26,000-acre park, situated on a site that was once a quarry in Northern California, the owner of this stunning home had one major theme in mind: clean, elegant lines that reflected inner peace.

This elegant home was designed by the architect to juxtapose the rough hewn surroundings with a serene and modern domicile.

The original home, built in the 1950s, had a beautiful setting but not much else to recommend it. The first order of business for designer Ken D'Andrea of Northbay Kitchen & Bath was to demolish the entire interior structure down to the studs. The next challenge was to reconfigure the interior walls to make room for an artist studio, bedrooms and a central hallway with vaulted ceilings, accented by skylights, running its entire length.

The construction of an addition gave the homeowner the kitchen and a living room with a hidden entertainment unit and vast views of a majestic oak and a garden filled with modern sculpture. The entire palate of pale greens and lightly stained maple cabinets reflects the lichen-covered oaks and granite boulders that surround this home with a quiet beauty. The slightly honed granite counters mirror the history of the site.

As a final detail, one of the boulders was incorporated into the glass panels of the entry, truly fulfilling the desire to bring the outside in.◆

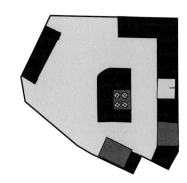

Special Features:
Verde Esmaralda granite counters; suspended shelves; hidden entertainment center; desk area; oversized island with cooktop.

Dimensions:
22.5' X 15'

Products Used:
Cabinetry: Dura Supreme Alectra Series
Flooring: Sawn Bleached Maple
Countertops: Slab Granite
Sink: Rohl Apron Front Fireclay
Faucets: Chicago
Dishwasher : Asko
Cooktop: 36" Thermador
Lighting: Recessed; Ambiance under cabinet
Refrigerator: 36" KitchenAid
Wallcovering: Multi layered faux finish
Oven: Thermador

DESIGNER

Ken D'Andrea
Northbay Kitchen & Bath
822 Petaluma Blvd. North
Petaluma, CA 94952
Phone: 707.769.1646

DESIGNER

Kristen Zwitt and Mike
Teipen, CMKBD
Kitchens by Teipen, Inc.
1035 N. State Road 135
Greenwood, IN 46142
317.888.7345

Photographer: Michael Teipen, CMKBD

Open space to display art pieces fits right in.

Special Features:
Custom hood with decorative tile and stucco finish; two workstations for multiple cooks; display areas; large walk-in pantry and Sub-Zero Refrigerator and Sub-Zero Freezer for catered dinners.

Dimensions:
24' X 17'

Products Used:
Cabinetry: Teipen Signature Cabinetry
Flooring: Plaza Colorado Rojo 13 X 13 tiles
Countertops: Corian, Terra
Sink: Corian, Bone
Faucets: Delta
Dishwasher: Asko
Range: Thermador
Lighting: Halo Recessed Cans & Wac Undercabinet & Accent Pucks
Refrigerator: Sub-Zero
Freezer: Sub-Zero
Wallcovering: Faux Finish
Warming Drawer: Thermador
Trash Compactor: KitchenAid
Microwave: KitchenAid
Wine Cooler: Sub-Zero
Double Ovens: Gaggenau
Hood Insert: Best

displaying
the art of renovation

The kitchen in this Spanish-style home needed to be redone not only to complement the exterior design elements but also to make it work better for the empty-nesters who love to cook and entertain frequently. The homeowners wanted a large kitchen with many appliances, as well as display areas for their many high-quality pieces of Southwestern art. The wall separating the dining room and kitchen was removed, the stair wall was opened halfway and the large built-in cabinets that obstructed the view into the large family room were demolished.

The design team, led by Kristen Zwitt and Mike Teipen, CMKBD, of Kitchens by Teipen Inc., specified twin Sub-Zeroes to eliminate the long walks to the older refrigerator/freezer in the garage. The large, open display area above and the matching wood fronts give this area a furniture look and open space to display

art pieces. A large built-in pantry houses more than enough cooking supplies. A wine cooler was positioned out of the main work area to avoid congestion while entertaining.

Stucco was added to the custom-made wood hood, and the walls and hood were faux finished by local craftsmen. The tile band around the hood complements the backsplash and floor tile to integrate this design element.◆

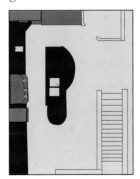

APPENDIX
KITCHEN TEMPLATES

Cabinets

| 6"x24" | 6"x24" | 6"x24" | 6"x24" | 6"x24" | 6"x24" | desk 36"x24" | desk 30"x24" | 9"x24" | 9"x24" | 9"x24" | 9"x24" | 9"x24" | 9"x24" | 9"x24" | 9"x24" |

| 12"x24" | 12"x24" | 12"x24" | 12"x24" | 12"x24" | 12"x24" | 12"x24" | 6"x24" | base cabinet 15"x24" | base cabinet 15"x24" | base cabinet 15"x24" | base cabinet 15"x24" | base cabinet 15"x24" | base cabinet 15"x24" | base cabinet 15"x24" | base cabinet 15"x24" |

| base cabinet 15"x24" | 9"x24" | 6"x24" | base cabinet 18"x24" | base cabinet 18"x24" | base cabinet 18"x24" | base cabinet 18"x24" | base cabinet 18"x24" | base cabinet 18"x24" | base cabinet 18"x24" | base cabinet 18"x24" | base cabinet 18"x24" | base cabinet 18"x24" | base cabinet 18"x24" |

| base cabinet 21"x24" | base cabinet 21"x24" | base cabinet 21"x24" | base cabinet 21"x24" | base cabinet 21"x24" | base cabinet 21"x24" | 9"x24" | base cabinet 24"x24" | base cabinet 24"x24" | base cabinet 24"x24" | base cabinet 24"x24" | base cabinet 24"x24" |

| base cabinet 24"x24" | base cabinet 24"x24" | base cabinet 24"x24" | base cabinet 24"x24" | base cabinet 24"x24" | 9"x24" | base cabinet 27"x24" | base cabinet 27"x24" | base cabinet 27"x24" | base cabinet 27"x24" | base cabinet 27"x24" |

| base cabinet 27"x24" | base cabinet 15"x24" | base cabinet 30"x24" | base cabinet 30"x24" | base cabinet 30"x24" | base cabinet 30"x24" | base cabinet 30"x24" | base cabinet 30"x24" | base cabinet 30"x24" | base cabinet 30"x24" |

| base cabinet 33"x24" | base cabinet 33"x24" | base cabinet 33"x24" | base cabinet 33"x24" | base cabinet 33"x24" | 12"x24" | base cabinet 36"x24" | base cabinet 36"x24" | base cabinet 36"x24" |

| base cabinet 36"x24" | base cabinet 36"x24" | base cabinet 36"x24" | base cabinet 36"x24" | base cabinet 36"x24" | base cabinet 36"x24" | base cabinet 39"x24" | base cabinet 39"x24" |

| base cabinet 39"x24" | base cabinet 39"x24" | base cabinet 39"x24" | base cabinet 42"x24" | base cabinet 42"x24" | base cabinet 42"x24" | base cabinet 18"x24" | base cabinet 18"x24" |

| base cabinet 42"x24" | base cabinet 45"x24" | base cabinet 45"x24" | base cabinet 45"x24" | base cabinet 45"x24" | base cabinet 45"x24" | base cabinet 45"x24" |

| base cabinet 45"x24" | left-hand corner-base cabinet 36"x24" | left-hand corner-base cabinet 36"x24" | left-hand corner-base cabinet 36"x24" | right-hand corner-base cabinet 36"x24" | right-hand corner-base cabinet 36"x24" | right-hand corner-base cabinet 36"x24" | right-hand corner-base cabinet 36"x24" |

Pantry Cabinets

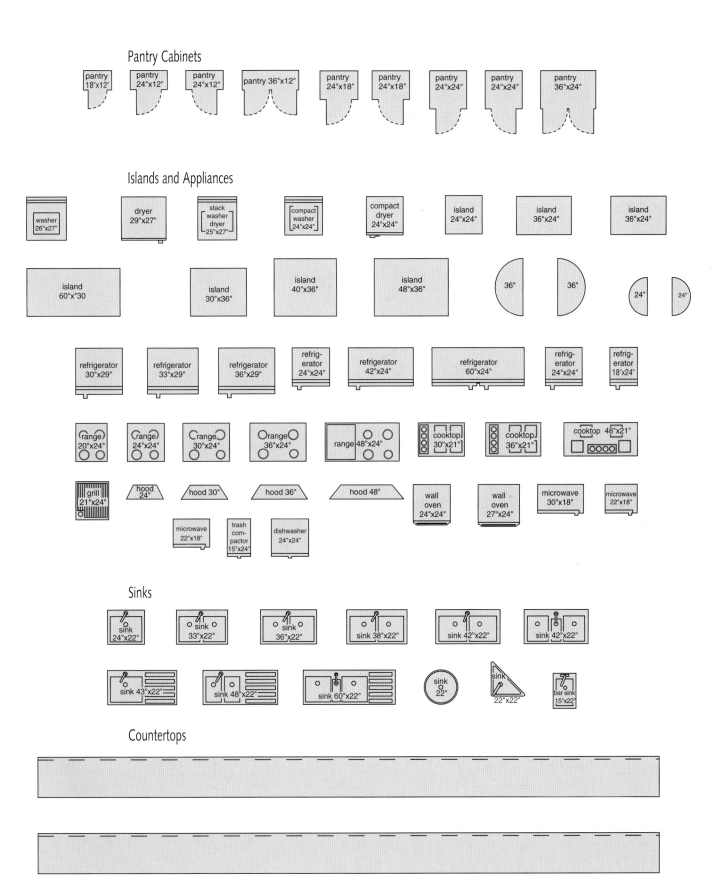

Islands and Appliances

Sinks

Countertops

Tables

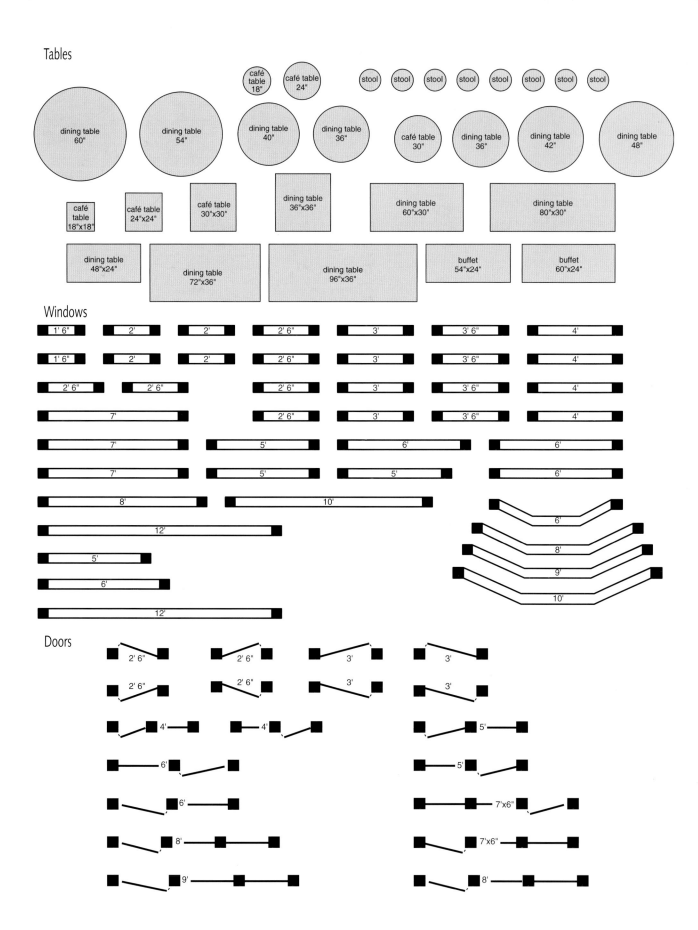

café table 18"

café table 24"

stool stool stool stool stool stool stool stool

dining table 60"

dining table 54"

dining table 40"

dining table 36"

café table 30"

dining table 36"

dining table 42"

dining table 48"

café table 18"x18"

café table 24"x24"

café table 30"x30"

dining table 36"x36"

dining table 60"x30"

dining table 80"x30"

dining table 48"x24"

dining table 72"x36"

dining table 96"x36"

buffet 54"x24"

buffet 60"x24"

Windows

1' 6" | 2' | 2' | 2' 6" | 3' | 3' 6" | 4'

1' 6" | 2' | 2' | 2' 6" | 3' | 3' 6" | 4'

2' 6" | 2' 6" | 2' 6" | 3' | 3' 6" | 4'

7' | 2' 6" | 3' | 3' 6" | 4'

7' | 5' | 6' | 6'

7' | 5' | 5' | 6'

8' | 10' | 6'

12' | 8'

5' | 9'

6' | 10'

12'

Doors

2' 6" | 2' 6" | 3' | 3'

2' 6" | 2' 6" | 3' | 3'

4' | 4' | 5'

6' | 5'

6' | 7'x6"

8' | 7'x6"

9' | 8'

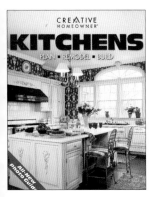
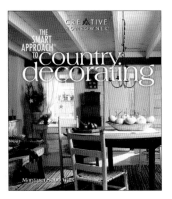
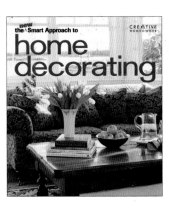

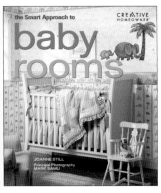

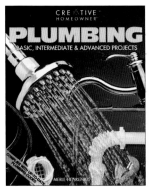
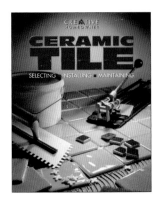